THE KOREAN
MANAGEMENT
SYSTEM

THE KOREAN MANAGEMENT SYSTEM

Cultural, Political, Economic Foundations

Chan Sup Chang
and Nahn Joo Chang

Q

Quorum Books
Westport, Connecticut • London

Library of Congress Cataloging-in-Publication Data

Chang, Ch' an-sŭp.
    The Korean management system : cultural, political, economic
foundations / Chan Sup Chang and Nahn Joo Chang.
     p.   cm.
    Includes bibliographical references and index.
    ISBN 0–89930–858–9
    1. Management—Korea (South) 2. Corporate culture—Korea (South)
3. Labor policy—Korea (South) 4. Korea (South)—Economic
conditions—1960–   I. Chang, Nahn Joo. II. Title.
HD70.K6C437 1994
658'.0095195—dc20   93–27710

British Library Cataloguing in Publication Data is available.

Library of Congress Catalog Card Number: 93–27710
ISBN: 0–89930–858–9

First published in 1994

Quorum Books, 88 Post Road West, Westport, CT 06881
An imprint of Greenwood Publishing Group, Inc.

Printed in the United States of America

The paper used in this book complies with the Permanent
Paper Standard issued by the National Information Standards
Organization (Z39.48–1984).

10 9 8 7 6 5 4 3 2

Copyright Acknowledgments

Chapter 6 is based on Chan Sup Chang, "Chaebol: The South Korean Conglomerates,"
Business Horizons (March-April 1988): 51–57. Copyright © 1988 by the Foundation for
the School of Business at Indiana University. Used with permission.

Chapter 7 is based on Chan Sup Chang, "Human Resource Management in Korea," in
Korean Management Dynamics, edited by Kae H. Chung and Hak Chong Lee. New
York: Praeger, 1989. Used with permission from Praeger Publishers, an imprint of
Greenwood Publishing Group, Inc., Westport, CT.

To

the loving memory of

Rev. and Mrs. Sung Sik Chang

and

to our two sons.

Contents

Tables and Figures

FIGURES

Preface

We approached the Korean management system from a cultural context. Although they share a common Oriental culture with other neighboring nations, Koreans maintain a unique culture. This culture, combined with the impact of the geopolitical environment of the Korean peninsula, results in a unique behavioral pattern. Thus, managers and workers in the Korean management system behave differently from their counterparts in other countries.

The Koreans have accomplished remarkable economic success since the 1960s, and their management system has played a major role in contributing to this phenomenal economic achievement. Entrepreneurs, top executives, managers, and workers in the management system are all integral parts of the system, and they have performed their assigned jobs effectively. Therefore, to comprehend the unique nature of this Korean management system, we performed an in-depth analysis on its performance.

The external environment of the Korean management system is a crucial factor in understanding it. In this kind of environment, the role of government is prominent because without active support from the government, no enterprise can survive and prosper. The government, in return, demands some favors from these enterprises, making this a quid pro quo, a unique feature of the Korean management system. We will discuss extensively the relationship between government and business to understand the Korean management system.

Because South Korea is a rapidly changing society, variable sources of information like newspapers and weekly and monthly magazines were integrated into this book. Of course, we also used books published in South Korea and elsewhere for developing a conceptual framework of the Korean management system. We acknowledge our appreciation to Lander University for granting one semester for sabbatical leave to one of us so that he was able to lay the groundwork for preparing this book. We were very persistent in preparing this book despite our full-time teaching obligations as undergraduate instructors.

Many people appear in this book—politicians, government officials, entrepreneurs, top executives, and managers. There are many ways of spelling their Korean names in English; we found eleven different spellings in English for one Korean family name. Nevertheless, we did our best to spell their names as they are spelled in English.

We believe that this book is unique in that it is one of the first books to lay a comprehensive conceptual framework for understanding the Korean management system. This book is also unique since it includes ethical issues in the Korean management system and we believe that it is the first such study published in the United States.

It is our sincere desire that readers of this book understand the Korean management system and its implication to other management systems. We, as Korean-Americans living in the United States for more than a quarter of a century, have experienced both Oriental and Western cultures. Thus, we are confident that we are able to comprehend the Korean management system more objectively than those who do not share this experience.

Introduction

According to a report of the International Bank for Reconstruction and Development (IBRD 1992), the South Korean economy achieved the highest GNP growth in the world for a quarter of a century (1965 to 1990), the average annual economic growth being an astonishing 7.1 percent. How could the Koreans have achieved such an impressive economic growth? Before the economic take-off, the Korean economy had remained one of the poorest economies in the world. We came to the United States from South Korea when the GNP per capita was barely $100.

We attribute this phenomenal achievement to the industrious Koreans. In government, technocrats effectively formulated and implemented the economic policy through five-year economic planning, and in business, entrepreneurs and managers boldly formulated and skillfully implemented business strategies for their enterprises. Their employees effectively transformed these business strategies into viable goods and services through long, hard working hours. As a whole, the Korean people have nurtured a society that empowered its people through its educational system, family system, and fierce competition despite adverse environmental situations of the Korean peninsula.

Understanding the Korean management system is a prerequisite to understanding the rapid economic growth in South Korea. Without an effective management system, no economy can achieve rapid economic growth. The management system in South Korea, therefore, must be effective, and the purpose of this book is to help the reader to understand it.

Management systems are functions of their own cultures. The Korean culture is unique, even though it shares certain features of Oriental culture with the Chinese and the Japanese. In this book, we emphasize the importance of examining the culture in order to understand a management system. While we admit that there are many paths to understanding the management system of a country, we maintain that the cultural approach is the most appropriate approach toward understanding the Korean management system, because the Korean culture has produced and nurtured its own.

This book, therefore, discusses the Korean management system in the context of Korean culture. In this management system, entrepreneurs, managers, and workers demonstrate their unique behavior and how it differs from behavior developed under other management systems, such as those of Japan and the United States. Korean behavior proves to be very productive, even though people from other countries and cultures may experience difficulties in understanding it.

To such people, the behavioral patterns of Koreans are certainly a mystery. A Thai newspaper reported a phenomenon of Korean behavior that the Thai people found difficult to understand (Friends when Examination Days 1991). On the day of the national college examination, a reporter from Thailand saw policemen in their cars picking up high school graduates who wanted to apply for colleges. The policemen drove them to the sites of the examination; if they had not, the college applicants might not have reached the examination sites on time because the Seoul area is one of the heaviest trafficked areas in South Korea. The reporter wondered how the policemen could be so friendly to students who were potentially violent demonstrators. However, this phenomenon does not puzzle the Koreans at all because they can tell instinctively when to confront a situation with violence or when to be friendly. Another mystery of Korean behavior about which foreign reporters wondered was that there were very few fatalities during the violent demonstrations by students and workers in South Korea. Of course, there were some fatalities among students and policemen, but these were very unusual cases in Korean society.

One Asian government requested the South Korean government's advice about how to handle violent demonstrations without bloodshed and fatalities. The Asian government was well aware of the aftermath of violent demonstrations in South Korea. However, this request was cordially denied by the South Korean government. No one can comprehend this Korean behavioral pattern without understanding that Koreans hate bloodshed and killing more than any other people in the world. Butchers were members of the lowest class of Korean society because they were the people who killed and dealt with blood everyday in their work.

However, it is not unusual for Korean people to exercise extreme behavior just short of bloodshed and fatalities. Most Koreans are well aware that they will not be killed for their extreme behavior. The behavior of Koreans in an organizational setting is confrontational, and this behavioral pattern must be understood in the context of their blood-shunning attitude. The observation of a foreign banker in Seoul, Korea reflects this confrontational behavior. He said, "Koreans can be bloody hard-nosed. Just look at the way they drive. They never let anyone else go in front of them" (Kristoff 1987).

Kristoff also mentions the remark of one foreign diplomat in Seoul about South Korea's go-for-broke bargaining style, in which compromise is often scorned as a sign of weakness. These foreign officials criticized only this one aspect of the Korean behavior. However, a few years later, labor strife was reduced by 27 percent in the first half of 1991 from that of the same period of the previous year (Economic Planning Board 1991), and Koreans settled their labor strife through dialogue and negotiations with management. Therefore, another aspect of the behavioral patterns of the Koreans is that they can tell when to confront and when to compromise.

The study of the Korean management system is sketchy, but some books and articles on the topic have been published by scholars in South Korea, Japan, the United States, and European countries. We will continue our study on the Korean management system for a better understanding of the system, but we believe that a conceptual framework of it has already been developed in this book.

Since we approached the Korean management system from a cultural context, Chapter 1 emphasizes an understanding of the Korean culture and in Chapter 2 we discuss the impact of Korea's unique geopolitical environment on the Korean peninsula. We also discuss in Chapter 3 the relationship between the government and business, a unique feature of the Korean management system. For economic growth, the government and business have maintained a supplementary and complementary relationship. This, in turn, has been integrated into the Korean management system. Without comprehending this relationship, no one can clearly understand the management system.

Chapter 4 discusses the role of Korean entrepreneurs. No Korean management system would exist without the entrepreneur who formulated and developed it. In one sense, the Korean management system is a function of the management styles of various entrepreneurs. By using the Korean management system, entrepreneurs have been the driving force of the South Korean economy.

Chapter 5 then focuses on comprehending the behavioral patterns of Koreans, which have been reflected in the Korean management system. The Koreans have demonstrated many unique features of behavior, although they have shared with the Chinese and the Japanese much of the Oriental cultural heritage. In fact, some Japanese scholars were amazed by the difference of behavioral patterns between the Japanese and the Koreans. We will discuss these differences. One of us chatted with a colleague who was visiting as an exchange professor from Great Britain. He was asked about the differences and similarities of the life and people in the United States and Great Britain. The Brit responded by saying that Americans are very friendly on initial contact and then become reserved later in the relationship. In contrast, English people are very reserved on initial contact, but become more friendly later. If his observation is valid, the difference in behavioral patterns must be reflected in the management systems of Great Britain and the United States. Therefore, it is imperative to comprehend behavioral patterns of people in order to understand a management system.

We claim that the *chaebol* is, in a sense, the Korean management system. According to the Fair Trade Commission (FTC) (1992), a chaebol is a conglomerate whose total assets amount to 400 billion won ($533 million at the exchange rate of $1 to 750 won). Without the chaebol, there might not be a Korean management system nor an economic miracle in South Korea. The chaebol therefore plays a crucial role in the Korean management system and chaebol groups, which are giant conglomerates by the South Korean standards, have redefined and refined it. In other words, the Korean management system owes much to the management styles of top executives of chaebol groups. Chapter 6 elaborates on the function of chaebol.

The effective use of human resources is a key to effective management. Therefore, if the Korean management has been effective, this should be attributed to effective human resource management. The Korean management of human resources has been as unique as the Korean management system. We studied the human resources management through macro and micro approaches by first discussing human resources management in the Korean management system as a whole in Chapter 7, and then by focusing on the human resources management system of a company in the Seoul area in Chapter 8.

The office of planning and control has played an important role in the Korean management system because people in the office have refined the original ideas of their entrepreneurs, analyzed them objectively, and implemented them for the growth of their organizations. These offices are think tanks in a real sense. Top executives of organizations depend on their advice and contributions for the direction of their organizations. In Chapter 9, we discuss the think-tank people in organizations to understand the Korean management system.

One of the best ways to identify our own uniqueness is to compare ourselves with others. By this process, we can detect similarities and differences between the entities compared. We use this method by comparing the Korean management system with those of Japan and the United States. We chose the Japanese management system simply because

Japan and Korea share features of the Oriental culture. This approach will disclose the unique features of the Korean management system as compared with others that have a similar cultural heritage. We focused on the potential differences between these two management systems. We selected the American management system just because it is a typical management system of Western culture, which is very different from that of the Oriental system. In Chapter 10, we tried to find both similarities and differences of managerial practice between these two management systems.

The employees play a vital part of the Korean management system, and we attribute its effectiveness to their loyalty, dedication, contributions, and working habits. These employees, of course, express their grievances, complaints, and unhappiness within the management system. The bitterness of the Korean workers, in particular, exploded after the June uprising of 1987 in violent labor strife. Therefore, in Chapter 11, we review employees' perceptions, behaviors, loyalty, dedication, and work habits to comprehend the Korean management system.

Social responsibility and ethical issues are very crucial matters in any management system. In Chapter 12, we will discuss social responsibility of business corporations and other nonbusiness organizations in the Korean management system. We have also included ethical issues since unethical corporate behavior prevails in the Korean management system. We analyze these ethical issues from the context of the Korean culture because we believe that ethical issues are its products.

The study of the Korean management system has never been highlighted in either the United States or other countries despite a phenomenal Korean economic growth and transformation of the country into a democracy. We attribute this lack of attention to the overshadowing of Korea for so long by Japan and China. However, we would like to quote an editorial statement by David C. Unger of *The New York Times:*

Americans often carelessly lump Korea with Japan, or assume its history began with the Korean War. But Koreans are acutely conscious of their long cultural and political traditions. It was through Korean craftsmen and scholars that an isolated Japan first learned of Chinese civilization. Korea established a unified state earlier than any present European country and maintained its unity and independence for a millennium, until 1910. (1992)

Korea became a colony of Japan in 1910, and Japanese colonialism lasted until the end of World War II in 1945. We believe that Korea in general and South Korea in particular deserve to be treated fairly. This book will contribute to the assessment of Korea through the Korean management system.

Many years ago, Norman Pearlstine wrote an interesting article in *Forbes:*

The Taiwanese are especially nervous about South Korea, which with twice its population has a bigger and cheaper labor supply. South Korea's growth rates in the past years have been higher than Taiwan's, and it has recently gained a big edge over Taiwan in trade with Mideast. Ask a Taiwanese businessman what he fears most, mainland China or South Korea? He is more likely than not to reply, "South Korea." (1978)

I am reminded of a dialogue with a Chinese in Taipei, Taiwan, several years ago. The young Chinese was working as an assistant at a convention where I was registering for a meeting, and I was surprised by his fluent Korean. He told me that his family had moved to South Korea after the Chinese Communists took over the country, and he had lived there ever since. His father was still running a Chinese restaurant in South Korea. This college-educated Chinese told me about a remark made by his father, a Chinese who had lived in South Korea for more than forty years: "Both Japanese and Koreans will play an important role in the future." As a Korean-American, I was surprised by this comment. His remark may or may not be valid.

While events occurring in Japan and China have been recognized in the United States, Korea and South Korea in particular have been treated like forgotten children. South Korea has never been considered seriously by government, business, media, or even academicians. However, we argue that South Korea deserves the attention of scholars and practitioners simply because it is becoming an influential nation in the global community. To comprehend Korea in general and South Korea in particular, more attention is needed.

Some unique features of the Korean management style have been used by United States corporations, which are owned by Korean corporations. Baum (1987) quoted two comments on the Korean management style. "The Koreans are more flexible than we are," commented a Japanese spokesperson for Hitachi America Ltd. An American manager remarked, "The Japanese are from a homogeneous society, so they are less accepting of anything that is not Japanese. Korea is a land of division, so the people are willing to listen and not get their feet stuck in concrete."

There was, however, a strong disagreement about Baum's interpretation of the Korean management system. Moskowitz (1987) emphasized that in the Korean management system there exists an extreme paternalism that emphasizes direct emotional ties and responsibility for employees, as well as the distinctly Korean cultural emphasis on openly emotional personal ties. He summarizes the Korean system as an authoritarian system.

We believe that the Korean management system has to be understood in the context of the behavioral patterns of Koreans, which were formulated by the Korean culture. This being a scholarly book, we try to provide a conceptual framework of the management system in South Korea and an analysis of management practices, while intensifying the readers' interest in the Korean management system.

REFERENCES

Baum, L. Korea's Newest Export: Management Style. *Business Week* (January 19, 1987).

Economic Planning Board. A Report on Labor Strife, 1991.

The Fair Trade Commission. *The Designated Large Enterprises in 1992*, 1992.

Friends when Examination Days, Enemy when Demonstration: A Myth. *The Dong-A Daily News* (December 18, 1991).

IBRD. *Social Development Index, 1991–1992*, 1992.

Kristoff, N. D. Sour Mood in Seoul. *The New York Times* (July 22, 1987).

Moskowitz, K. Korean Management: More Feudal and Fraternal. *Business Week* (March 2, 1987).

Pearlstine, N. A Nation of Ostriches. *Forbes* (August 7, 1978).

Unger, D. C. Success, the Anxiety, in Korea: Editorial Notebook. *The New York Times* (January 23, 1992).

1

Korean Culture

As mentioned in the introduction, a management system is a function of its culture. This means that the culture of a nation influences and systematizes the management system of that nation. Understanding Korean culture, therefore, is a prerequisite to understanding the Korean management system.

Figure 1.1 (p. 10) shows the basic conceptual framework of the Korean management system in terms of the Korean culture. Korea, like Japan and the other countries surrounding China, has been under the influence of the Chinese culture for more than a thousand years. The Chinese culture, therefore, has dominated the Korean society and their everyday lives through political, legal, and social systems in addition to literature, religion, and ethics. Specifically, Chinese culture in general and the religions of Buddhism, Confucianism, Shamanism, and Taoism in particular have played an important role in Korea. Chinese language and literature are very important in that Chinese characters were used exclusively in Korea until the middle of the fifteenth century, and they are still used even after "hangul," the Korean alphabet, was introduced and used extensively. All aspects of the Chinese culture spread into Korea through Chinese books, traditions, customs, and the value system.

One out of four South Koreans is a Christian. The largest church in the world, with a congregation numbering at least half a million, is located in Seoul, and many influential leaders and managers both in business and nonbusiness organizations are dedicated Christians. Nevertheless, we exclude Christianity from the following discussion, because the Christian Church has only one hundred years of history in South Korea, except for the Catholic Church, and it may not yet have a profound impact on the formation of characteristics of the Korean people. Actually, Korean Christians are sometimes also believers of Buddhism,

Figure 1.1
Framework of the Korean Management System

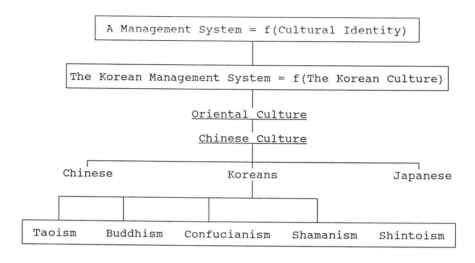

Confucianism, Shamanism, and Taoism in the sense that these four religions and teachings are integral parts of the Korean culture. We do not discuss Islam because there are only a few believers.

Although Buddhism and Confucianism have been generally accepted as religions in Korea and have become an integral part of the lives of the Koreans, there is a major difference between them: Buddhism is understood and practiced as a pure religion, and it recognizes heaven, hell, and transmigration. It teaches that anyone can enjoy the life of heaven if he or she has a virtuous and honest life in this world. Heaven is the reward for what anyone has done on earth. Buddhism, therefore, represents honest and virtuous living to Koreans.

Confucianism, as originally observed in China, is understood more as a moral philosophy with moral teachings than as a religion. It is involved more in the contemporary world, rather than emphasizing the afterlife. Having a meaningful, moral, and virtuous life in this world is an end itself; it does not serve as a precondition to the life after death. Confucianism, therefore, is not seriously concerned with the supernatural world, even though it recognizes the supernatural as an unknown world.

Koreans believe that they must fulfill an additional obligation of filial piety to their ancestors. Shamanism has been integrated into the lives of the Koreans through ancestor worship. Koreans, as living offspring, accept blessings in return from the spirits of their ancestors. It is really a quid pro quo. Shamanism recognizes the existence of various gods everywhere who possess the power to bless people who in turn seek the gods' blessing by their devoted prayers for their family members only. During the college entrance examination period, for example, mothers of college applicants fervently pray in Buddhist temples and Christian churches that the colleges will accept their children. This practice can be traced originally to Shamanism tradition, although the practitioners may be Buddhists, Christians, Confucians, or Taoists.

The practice of Shamanism in Korea shows the importance of the family system, which was emphasized and integrated fully into the teachings of Confucianism. Koreans are one of the most family-oriented people in the world. Maintaining family tradition and enhancing family prestige are the most important obligations to each family member. Although Korean Christians formally discontinue this process of Shamanism ritual, they still maintain informally the tradition of ancestor worship.

Through Chinese Taoism, Koreans conceived of the universe as a great hierarchical whole composed of parts, spaces, and times that correspond to one another. This whole, however, is not static. All entities, including human beings, are subject to changes and transformations (Eliade 1987). Believers in Taoism emphasize a distaste for worldly affairs and a yearning for life in harmony with nature.

We can see the uniqueness of Taoism when we compare Taoism with Confucianism. Taoism stresses avoiding conventional social obligations and leading a simple, spontaneous, and meditative life close to nature. By contrast, Confucianism emphasizes a well-disciplined society and stresses ceremony, duty, and public service. The Koreans have lived by these two different ideals. On the one hand, the Koreans try to succeed in the society following the tradition of Confucianism. On the other hand, Koreans downgrade the significance of worldly success and develop a fatalistic view of the world.

Nobody understands the Korean management system clearly without understanding the importance of the family system. Koreans work for their business mainly to preserve their family tradition and to enhance their family prestige through successful businesses. They also work for their business by becoming recognized managers and leaders. Through the ancestor-worship ritual, the living offspring proudly report to their ancestors of their success and thank the spirits for their blessings.

As was mentioned above, the teachings and the value system of Confucianism have prevailed in the minds of Koreans. This means that Confucianism has been accepted as a set of moral teachings and ethical values, but not as a religion. Based on Confucianism, the Korean society has the following characteristics:

1. Orderly Society
   a. Understanding and maintaining your position in society

2. Free Society
   a. No religious caste system
   b. No food restrictions except for health reasons
   c. Capability and determination determine your ultimate rank
3. Family-Oriented Society
   a. Filial piety to your parents
   b. Loyalty to superiors
   c. Paternalistic society
4. Group-Oriented Society
   a. Individualism in a group setting
   b. "Hwa" (harmony) among members
5. Education-Oriented Society
   a. Career success = f (level of education) mentality
   b. Respect for scholars

In any nation, Confucianism emphasizes a stable society based on loyalty to the state and superiors and filial piety to living parents and even to deceased ancestors through ancestor worship. It also stresses good relations among the members of the society by maintaining adequate hierarchical and lateral relationships. There is a strict hierarchical order to obey in that subordinates must respect and obey their superiors. This has an implication to the Korean management system that we will call the "Principle of Strict Hierarchical Order." On the other hand, superiors must protect the well-being and interests of their subordinates. This principle has a significant impact on the Korean management system, and we will call it the "Principle of Reciprocity." In summary, according to Confucianism, the ethical standards of a society are mutual trust and respect.

Traditionally, a stable society functions within the framework of a hierarchical social class system. The four classes of Confucian society were expressed by four Chinese characters. While Koreans pronounce these characters as "sa," "nong," "kong," and "sang," the Japanese pronounce them as "si," "no," "ko," and "sho." The top class of "sa" meant the literate class in Korea, but it also referred to the warrior class in Japan. The second highest class was the farmers; third, the manufacturers. The merchants were relegated to the bottom class because Korean people, in particular, understood that the merchant class exploited people by unjustifiable profit-taking.

It should be noted, however, that the divisions among these social classes were never as rigid and exclusive as those in the caste system in India—there was upward mobility in Korea. Unless someone belonged to the underclass, such as a serf or a man of very humble birth, he could rise to any level depending on talent, capacity, and family status. Yet the top class of "sa" enjoyed the most opportunities in Korea. This has an implication to Korean management that we will call the "Principle of Open Society."

In Confucian society, the importance of education cannot be overly emphasized, even today. In Korea, educated men or scholars have been highly respected. However, many Koreans could enjoy the privileges and status of the highest class of "sa" by passing the rigorous civil service examination, "kwageo," to become civil servants. In order to pass the examination, candidates prepared themselves for Confucian literature and politics. This implies that education was critically important to many Koreans since it determined success or failure in their career paths. The critical importance of education has an implication to the Korean management system that we will call the "Principle of Education Priority."

Koreans place greater importance on filial piety to parents than on piety to superiors, but the Japanese give higher priority to the reverse order (Hirschmeier and Yui 1981). Although the Korean society has emphasized loyalty to superiors and to the state, filial piety has been the most important form of social behavior. This means that the family system or family prestige has been the primary objective in Korea. In no other society do we find such a strict regulation to maintain the purity of the family system as in Korea. For example, with few exceptions, no one can marry a person who happens to have the same family name, and every household keeps its own genealogical table to identify the roots of its family.

The Korean family system is also unique in that it is defined in a very narrow and strict sense. That is, the system demands a more blood-oriented family than in other societies. The practice of adopting a son has never been used extensively in Korea. Each man must have his own son(s) by any means. If a man fails to have his own son, his last resort is to adopt a son from one of his brothers. Any married woman who cannot conceive a child is considered the most profound sinner and encounters much contempt in society. On February 12, 1988, NBC's *Today Show* reported about an adoption of children from South Korea. Two Korean brothers were sent to an orphanage because their step-father never accepted them as his children since they were not related by blood to him. Babies of unwed mothers have never been warmly accepted in Korean society and have ended up in orphanages where they might be adopted by American parents.

The strangely unique patrimonial heritage of the North Korean Communist system can be understood in this context. President Kim Il Sung is in the process of transferring his power structure to his son, Kim Jong Il. This case represents a complete departure from the typical Communist pattern as an application of the traditional Korean family system.

This practice still prevails in the Korean management system. Many Korean corporations are managed by members of the founder's families even after they have expanded into giant businesses. We will call this practice the "Principle of the Blood-oriented Family System."

Agriculture was accepted as the basic industry in Korea, and the status of farmers was recognized accordingly, although farmers were exploited by members of the top class. On the other hand, the status of manufacturers and artisans was very low in a society where agriculture was the dominant industry, and thus the manufacturing industry remained at the stage of pre-Industrial Revolution until the early twentieth century.

Merchants belonged to the lowest class in Korea. Their functions as transaction facilitators in society were not properly recognized. Instead, they were regarded as men of exploitation and profits. This bad connotation prompted an implication to the Korean management system which we will call the "Principle of Ignoring Commerce." This principle has had a negative impact on the Korean management system, but it has been modified extensively over the past thirty years.

You may wonder why Koreans failed to modernize their country as Japan did in 1868 through the Meiji Restoration if Koreans shared a common cultural heritage for so many years with the Japanese. This issue is beyond the scope of this book to discuss in detail, but identification of some of the key reasons is very important in order to understand the unique features of the Korean management system.

The main reasons lie in the unique lifestyle that Koreans had practiced. Their lifestyle stems from the unique personalities of Koreans, geopolitical impact, and sociocultural system. Since the Korean peninsula was surrounded by the major powers of China, Japan, and Russia, Koreans abandoned the policy of relying on military power to protect their independence. Instead, Korea was under the umbrella of Chinese protection. Militarism thus never gained any popularity in Korea, and Korean military men were never respected. There was no need to develop any huge logistic system for military operations that needed the help of the merchant class, who in other countries, flourished by providing supplies for military logistics. No serious connection between the military and merchants ever evolved in Korea; therefore, the merchant class had no opportunity to grow under such a nonmilitary and agrarian society. There is another reason: Since no priority was given to militarism in Korea, there was no incentive to develop modern weapon systems. Furthermore, there was no interaction between Koreans and Westerners until the nineteenth century.

Japan followed a different course. Since militarism was important in Japan, the warriors, called the samurai class, were genuinely interested in strengthening their military positions. The two most important requirements to meet this need were to develop a well-organized logistic system and to acquire the most advanced weapons. The former need had contributed to the development of the merchant class and the interaction between these two polarized classes. The samurai class depended on merchants for the effective management of their logistic system for wars, and the merchants depended on the samurai class for their safety and profits. From the early days, there was a close relationship between samurai and merchant classes. Thus commerce expanded rapidly in Japan.

The warriors' endeavor to have access to the most advanced weapons in Japan also had a great impact on the development of commerce in Japan. After Portuguese sailors became the first Europeans to reach Japan in 1543 (Takagi and Fukuda 1971), the Japanese warriors recognized that Westerners had developed more advanced weapon systems. Since then, the Japanese were interested in interacting with Westerners, although they kept an official policy of ostracism. Their interest in Western culture was highlighted in the so-called Dutch studies (Takagi and Fukuda 1971). Through the Dutch, who were in Japan for various reasons, the Japanese extensively studied advanced Western learning in many fields other than just weaponry. They adapted useful ideas more effectively than any other Asian nation. Japan, therefore, never closed her doors completely to foreigners except during certain periods. This access to Western culture was one of the driving forces for the restoration movement of 1868 in Japan, and it also partially explains why Japan became the first nation in Asia to undergo such a movement.

On the contrary, interaction between Koreans and Westerners was quite limited. China was the only country with which Korea had extensive relations and trade, including tribute. Koreans considered anything related to China admirable. By contrast, trade with Japan was not prosperous and took place only intermittently.

Koreans interacted with Westerners when shipwrecked Dutch sailors landed on the Korean coast in 1628 and 1653 (Han 1989), but Korean officials never took advantage of these opportunities. There were also other occasions to interact with Westerners in the sixteenth and seventeenth centuries, but Koreans refused to use such opportunities for their benefit.

Unfortunately, Western learning never had any significant impact on Korea until the arrival of Roman Catholic Church missionaries during the latter part of the eighteenth century. As a result, Korea remained one of the most secluded countries for many years until foreign powers forced the Korean government to open her doors in the latter part of the nineteenth century. A commercial treaty was signed in 1876 with Japan, and similar treaties were arranged in 1882 with the United States and then China. Korea had followed China's leadership closely for so many years that her government was not flexible enough to make independent decisions for the country.

You cannot understand the Korean culture and people until you comprehend the yin–yang concept. The Korean people perceive the universe in terms of dual cosmic forces. One force represents a positive aspect; the other represents a negative aspect. For example, sun, male, spring, sunny spot, day, and odd numbers belong to yang (positive); moon, female, fall, shady spot, night, and even numbers belong to yin (negative). The Koreans were so fanatic about this dualism that they expressed their sentiment on their national flag. The South Korean flag has a circle in the center with a dividing line, which represents the yin–yang concept.

Through this yin–yang concept, the Koreans perceive differences in the universe: between sun and moon, male and female, spring and fall, sunny spot and shady spot, and odd numbers and even numbers. However, they also perceive the complementary nature of these differences, for example, between male and female. Nothing is complete unless these pairs match each other and function accordingly. Each element in a positive/negative pair needs the other to become a complete substance: A male needs a female, the sun needs the moon, and the spring needs the fall. Through this matching process, these pairs fulfill a synergistic effect. In the yin–yang concept, the coexistence between different pairs is a requirement.

Understanding this difference–complement dichotomy is essential to understanding the Oriental culture and the Korean culture. It has one important distinction: A sense of hatred because one sees a difference, but no sense of conquest, destruction, or enmity can develop because a part needs the other part as complement. The other part must be cherished, not destroyed. In this world of yin–yang, there also is no value system. The moon is as important as the sun, because we need night as well as we need day. In one sense, yin–yang is a value-free and doctrine-free concept.

To the Korean people, the dualism of God and the devil is an alien and unfamiliar perception. A god and a devil, of course, are different, but they are not complementary to each other. Devils as threatening evils must be conquered or destroyed. This is a holy war. A god-abiding person cannot accept, tolerate, or coexist with a devil-abiding person. God-abiding people must prevail throughout. We cannot simply accept the existence of a devil-dominated world. The evil world must be destroyed or conquered. This is really a zero-sum game.

The yin–yang concept has a great implication to the Korean management system through Korean culture and behavior of the Korean people. You can see peaceful coexistence of various religions in South Korea, but there has never been extensive interaction among them. No religion has ever developed a perception that other religions are evil and must, therefore, be conquered or destroyed. A concept of holy religious war has never developed against other religions in Korea.

This brings some uncomfortable feelings among Korean Christians who have been indoctrinated that Christianity is the only religion that does not recognize the existence of any gods of other religions. In church, the Korean Christians behave exactly like real Christians. Outside church, they transform themselves into Korean Christians who unwillingly acknowledge the existence of other religions and the yin–yang concept of different but complementary relationships. In one sense, Korean Christians live in two different worlds: a world of no compromise, and a world of compromise and complement. The Korean Christians are really yin–yang Christians who have to reconcile their Korean cultural heritage with Christian doctrines. They believe in Buddhism, Confucianism, and Shamanism as mentioned before; therefore, they practice Christianity in a culture that inherited and cherished the values of teachings of various religions and philosophies.

To Korean Christians, ecumenism has a different meaning from that to a Westerner. It is a movement among different religions in addition to a movement among different denominations of the Christian church. Some scholars defend the dialogue between Christianity and Confucianism. In the conference meeting of The Korean Society for Religious Study in North America, some Korean-American scholars presented papers on the necessity of a dialogue between the two religions. Scholars argued that some common ground can be found between Christianity and Confucianism.

During the Korean presidential election campaign in 1992, three major presidential candidates attended an important Buddhist ritual because they needed to court the votes of Buddhists, which is the largest religious group in South Korea. Kim Young Sam is a Presbyterian elder; Kim Dae Jung is a Catholic; and Chung Ju Yung does not belong to any religious group. As a church elder, Kim Young Sam complied with the Buddhist ritual without violating his Christian practice. As a devout Catholic, Kim Dae Jung did not comply significantly with the ritual. As presidential candidates, they must be extremely careful not to alienate themselves from Buddhist believers in order to court their votes. Chung Ju Yung, free from any religious restrictions, participated in the ritual without reservations. The example of these presidential candidates demonstrates a typical behavioral pattern of Koreans: accommodating their culture and their religious practices.

In conclusion, the Korean management system shares many features with other management systems. However, it is unique in the sense that the Korean culture has its distinctive features, and a management system is a function of its own culture. Of course, Korean people share the

Chinese culture with the Chinese and the Japanese. Still, Koreans have developed a unique cultural pattern different from that of both China and Japan. In this chapter, we also investigated some of the probable reasons why Korea failed to modernize its country and its economy as Japan did in the nineteenth century. The difference may be attributed to cultural nuances and geopolitical factors. The latter is the subject of the next chapter.

REFERENCES

Eliade, M. (ed.). *Encyclopedia of Religion.* Vol. 14. New York: Macmillan Publishing Company, 1987.

Han, W. K. *Hankuk Tongsa* (History of Korea). Seoul: Ulyu Moonhwasa, 1989.

Hirschmeier, J. and Yui, T. *The Development of Japanese Business, 1600–1980.* 2d ed. London and Boston: George Allen & Unwin, 1981.

Takagi, K. and Fukuda, M. (eds.). *Nihonno Rekishi* (History of Japan). Vols. 2–3. Tokyo: Yomiuri Shinbunsha, 1971.

2

Geopolitical Environment

The geopolitical environment of any country has a great impact on its political independence and economic growth. The collapse of the Soviet Union and subsequent declaration of independence of three Baltic countries—Estonia, Latvia, and Lithuania—have vividly demonstrated the profound impact of a geopolitical environment on the survival of a nation. The North American Free Trade Agreement (NAFTA) between Canada, the United States, and Mexico is another example of the impact of geopolitical environment. Because of the geographical proximity, these three countries endeavor to achieve the common goal of economic prosperity through cooperation and free trade.

Korea has never been an exception. The major powers, which consist of China, Japan, Russia, and, to some extent, the United States, have maintained interest in the Korean peninsula. During the late nineteenth century, the Korean government tried desperately to maintain the independence of the country in the midst of the power struggles among China, Japan, and Russia. But Korea failed to prevent foreign encroachment and was annexed eventually by Japan in 1910, thus becoming a colony of Japan until the end of World War II.

The Koreans lost these valuable forty years (1905–1945) to Japan and missed the golden opportunity of modernizing their country with their own initiatives and directions. During these humiliating and suppressive long years, the catchwords of the Koreans were "kukkwon hoibok" meaning restoration of national independence. In order to achieve this goal, the Korean leaders recognized that promoting education and industry by Koreans was the only necessary course of action. This effort, of course, encountered severe suppression from the Japanese rulers since the major colonial policy of the Japanese military-dominated government in Korea was to deny education to Koreans and industrialization

Table 2.1
Authorized Capital by Nationality and Industry at the End of 1940

(Unit: thousand yen)

Industry	Koreans		Japanese	
	Amount	Ratio	Amount	Ratio
Printing and Publishing	1,500	43%	2,000	57%
Metals	6,100	2	373,000	98
Machinery	61,000	42	85,050	58
Chemicals	1,000	–	276,250	100
Electricity and gas	–	–	553,030	100
Ceramic or Pottery	–	–	53,245	100
Textiles	14,000	14	76,600	86
Lumber	5,500	10	47,000	90
Food processing	5,250	7	73,800	93
Others	7,000	8	83,500	92
Total	101,350	6	1,623,475	94

Source: The Bank of Korea, *The Economic Yearbook*, 1948.

Table 2.2
Number of Korean Engineers

Industry	Total (A)	Koreans (B)	B/A
Metals	1,214	133	11%
Machinery	609	150	25
Chemicals	2,004	222	11
Gas, Electric, Water	991	190	19
Ceramics	245	48	20
Textiles	484	132	27
Lumber	99	32	32
Food processing	336	121	36
Printing	56	24	43
Construction	2,347	551	23
Others	91	29	32
Total	8,476	1,632	19%

Source: The Bank of Korea, *The Economic Yearbook*, 1948.

by Koreans. Although the Japanese allowed Korean children to receive elementary and secondary education, the opportunity for higher education to Koreans was severely restricted. The Japanese rulers also imposed various limitations upon Koreans in their efforts to build industries. For example, Koreans were restricted from operating in heavy industry and were allowed to run a few factories in consumer goods or light industry. Thus, only a handful of Koreans managed to become entrepreneurs.

Table 2.1 demonstrates strikingly the discrimination against Koreans by the Japanese rulers in Korea. Table 2.2 shows the number of Korean engineers under Japanese control at the end of 1944. The colonial control of the Japanese over the Korean people had a profoundly adverse impact upon the growth of the Korean economy. First of all, the Japanese strategy of pursuing their objectives resulted in an unbalanced structure of industry in Korea. The heavy industry was located primarily in the northern part of the country, and the light or consumer goods industries were concentrated in the South. This industrial structure gave a tremendous disadvantage to South Korea vis-à-vis North Korea for restructuring the economy after World War II. In addition, Korean businessmen were not allowed to manage heavy industry so they concentrated only on consumer goods industries. Second, the Japanese control resulted in the critical shortage of skilled Korean manpower, which hindered the economic reconstruction of both North and South Korea after World War II.

Of course, the Japanese government made some positive contributions in Korea. The Japanese transformed Korea into a modern society. They modernized the education, transportation, communication, economic, and government systems. Sometimes the growth rates in the Korean economy outpaced those of Japan. According to Cumings (1991), recent research has indicated that the annual growth rate of Korea was 3.6 percent in the period 1911–1938, while that of Japan was only 3.4 percent.

The surrender of the Japanese to the Allied Forces brought liberation to the Korean people, who breathed freedom for the first time after almost forty years of colonial bondage. However, misfortune hit Koreans again. This time, the United States and the former Soviet Union divided Korea in half.

After World War II, the American military government reigned in South Korea until the South Koreans could establish their own government on August 15, 1948. In the North, a Communist government was established in the same year with the help of the former Soviet military. The Korean economy was in disarray because all the Japanese had left the country, and few Koreans had the skills to manage the economy. While goods became scarce, inflation soared. The Korean people became disillusioned by all their hardships following the liberation.

By comparing the economy of the two years, 1941 and 1948, we can

Table 2.3
Devastation of the Korean Economy

Industry	Number of Factories			Number of Employees		
	1941	1948	Change	1941	1948	Change
Textiles	1,301	1,325	+2.0%	54,000	54,177	+0%
Chemicals	517	767	+48.4	17,369	24,857	+43
Food processing	1,863	646	-65.3	25,182	5,227	-79
Machinery	585	548	-7.2	14,825	8,971	-39
Metals	408	206	-49.5	9,393	4,362	-54
Printing	371	72	-80.0	7,498	1,897	-75
Ceramics	366	115	-68.6	6,345	4,628	-27
Industrial arts	971	134	-86.2	14,580	1,777	-89

Source: The Bank of Korea, The Monthly Survey, no. 46 (June, 1959), p. 10.

see the devastation of the Korean economy after World War II. Table 2.3 demonstrates that the South Korean economy withered under the American military government. Meanwhile, the military government implemented a massive aid program to feed Koreans and to sustain the economy. Altogether, the South Korean people received $494 million in grant under Government and Relief in the Occupied Area (GARIOA) and $24.5 million until the establishment of the South Korean government in 1948 (Koh, H. S., Kim, K. S., and Um, K. Y. 1969).

Another deadly tragedy rocked the peninsula when the Korean Conflict broke out on June 25, 1950. The South Korean economy became almost totally paralyzed, and industry was heavily damaged. For example, the war destroyed 26 percent of the metal industry, 35 percent of the machinery industry, 64 percent of the textile industry, 33 percent of the chemical industry, 20 percent of the ceramic industry, and 75 percent of the printing industry (Lee 1983).

On July 27, 1953, the Korean Conflict ended with the truce agreement between the United Nations forces and the North Korean and Chinese Communist countries. Since then, the citizens of the Republic of Korea (South Korea) strived to reconstruct their wartorn economy. This reconstruction effort set a foundation for their future economic growth in the 1960s and 1970s. Once again, the aid from the United States played a crucial role in South Korea's recovery. The United Nations Korean Reconstruction Agency (UNKRA), the International Cooperation Agency (ICA), the Economic Cooperation Administration (ECA), the Civil Relief in Korea (CRIK), and the aid program of the Public Law 480 were the

Table 2.4
American Aid and the GNP

Year	GNP (billion won)	U.S. Aid ($ million)	U.S. Aid/GNP (%)
1953	86.85	194.2	11.2
1954	91.35	153.9	8.4
1955	95.02	236.7	12.4
1956	95.28	326.7	17.1
1957	103.53	382.9	18.5
1958	110.70	321.3	14.5
1959	116.48	222.2	9.5

Source: The Bank of Korea, The Saving Accounts in South Korea, 1961, p. 9.
Note: The GNP was the constant value of 1955; we translated the U.S. dollar to Korean won in order to calculate the ratio of the U.S. aid and the GNP in South Korea.

main sources of assistance from the United States. Between 1945 and 1970 (Krueger 1979), the Republic of Korea (South Korea) received $5.168 billion of aid from the United States. The aid constituted an important portion of the Gross National Product (GNP) of South Korea, as Table 2.4 shows.

The end of the Cold War and the collapse of the Communist system shook up the entire world, which was seeking a new world order. The atmosphere of this new world order will have a tremendous impact on the Korean peninsula in which South Korea had been the most unyielding non-Communist country in the world while North Korea still insists on the legitimacy of the strict Communist idealogy. However, dialogues between South and North Korea for eliminating hatred and mistrust are welcome indications for the reunification of both North and South Korea.

Here again the geopolitical environment will play a critical role in unifying Korea. The big powers of China, Japan, Russia, and the United States once again will have a great impact on this matter. Their interests may conflict with the desire of the Korean people. If so, reunification is out of the question regardless of the Koreans' wishes. If they recognize that the stability of one Korea is conducive to their own interests, then the reunified Korea will eventually be realized. The Korean people anticipate that by the end of this century they will become citizens of the unified government in the Korean peninsula.

In this geopolitical environment of Korea, three nations have had a significant impact on Koreans and the Korean management system. For more than a thousand years, China has influenced the lives of Koreans through the Chinese culture, the backbone of the Oriental culture. Every aspect of the Korean culture is a replica of the Chinese culture in the Korean peninsula. It is really a wonder that Koreans have maintained their own unique culture amid the overwhelming encroachment of the Chinese culture.

China has also had a tremendous impact on the Korean management system through the Confucian value system, which has provided a basic value system for the Korean management system. It has also laid a foundation for the organizational hierarchy through loyalty to superiors and interpersonal relationships and through "hwa" or harmony.

Japan also has had a great impact on Koreans and the Korean management system. The Japanese occupation of Korea for almost forty years was very tragic for Koreans. Koreans were deprived of their independence and were totally at the mercy of the Japanese authorities for their daily lives and future destinations. Koreans still resent having been under the Japanese control from 1910 to 1945. However, the Japanese brought about the modernization of Korea, although it was for their own interests and not for the sake of the Koreans. Regardless of the Japanese motives, this modernization process has had a significant impact on the Korean management system.

Organizational structures in Korea are really duplications of those of Japan. Koreans call a company "hoisa," which originated from "kaisha" in Japan. Both of them are written by using the same Chinese characters. The Japanese pronounce them as kaisha, and the Koreans as hoisa. On the other hand, the Chinese call a company "kungszu" and use different Chinese characters.

The titles of an organizational hierarchy in South Korea originated in Japan; they are the same Chinese characters, but the Japanese and the Koreans pronounce them differently. In other words, both countries use the same Chinese characters for titles from the chairman of the board of trustees, to the president, all the way down to the staff. Koreans have accepted these terms as their own, and they seem to have no regret.

Since the end of World War II, the United States has had an enormous influence upon the lives of Koreans and the Korean management system. Koreans owed Americans for their livelihood and survival during the American military government period (1945–1948) and during and after the Korean Conflict (1950–1960s). In addition, the Americans brought advanced technology and knowledge of the American (Western) civilization to South Korea.

Since it was introduced to business schools in universities and colleges in South Korea in the early 1960s, the American business system has been extensively studied by both scholars and students. In those days, the business education in South Korea was really an imitation of that of the

United States. In many cases, American textbooks were used in college classrooms in South Korea without any significant modification.

While the dominant American system failed to produce a fundamental change in the Korean management system, the former has had a powerful impact on the latter. Nevertheless, the Korean management system remains as an Oriental management system, unique from other management systems, such as those of Japan and the United States.

The geopolitical environment of Korea has had a great impact upon Koreans in every aspect of their lives. The Korean management system is no exception to this statement. The major outside players in the Korean geopolitical environment have been China, Japan, and the United States. These three countries have had an extraordinary impact upon the Korean management system. Next, we will discuss the relationship between the government and business. This relationship will explain another unique feature of the Korean management system.

REFERENCES

Cumings, B. *The Two Koreas.* Hardline Series. New York: The Foreign Policy Association, Inc., 1991.

Koh, H. S., Kim, K. S., and Um, K. Y. (eds.). *Hapdong Yonkam (Yearbook).* Hapdong Tongshinsa, 1969.

Krueger, A. O. *The Development Role of the Foreign Sector and Aid.* Cambridge, Mass.: Council on East Asian Studies, Harvard University, 1979.

Lee, H. J. *Hanil Bikyo Kyungjesaron* (Economic Histories of Korea and Japan: A Comparative Approach). Seoul: Bibong Chulpansa, 1983.

3

Government and Business

Governments formulate their policies according to national goals or aspirations. If any country aspires toward healthy economic growth and modernization, government policies must be formulated and implemented accordingly. Businessmen must also respond and act appropriately.

As mentioned before, the Korean people failed to experience a restoration movement in the nineteenth century as did the Japanese during the Meiji Restoration of 1868. However, Korean leaders, inside and outside the government, attempted to initiate such a movement, modeled after the Meiji Restoration with the catchword of "kaehwa," meaning modernization or enlightenment (of Korea). The intervention of the major powers of China, Russia, and Japan jeopardized this effort. Moreover, the mood for modernization was not ripe in Korea. However, the Korean government still attempted to modernize the country despite such an adverse environment. King Ko Jong (Cho 1974) established the Bureaus of Arsenal and Mint in 1883, the Bureau of Textile in 1855, and the Bureau of Paper Production and Mines in 1887. Each bureau had its own factory to produce goods. This was the king's effort to promote industries in Korea. In this regard, his aspiration did not produce satisfactory results because of many obstacles both inside and outside Korea.

The civilian leaders also realized the necessity of modernization for the sake of the nation's survival. For example, Yu Kil Jun (1856–1916) published a 555-page book *Seoyu Kyunmungi, (A Record of What I Saw and Heard in the West)* in 1895 (Korean Overseas Information Service 1979). In his book, he urged Korea to modernize along the lines many Western countries were following to achieve their goals. Yu also wrote an article entitled "Company Charters" in 1882 and another article, "The Introduction of the Joint Stock Company," in 1883. Both were considered the first articles on the company system in Korea. Although Yu himself was not a businessman, he recognized the importance of building industries for Korea's survival and prosperity. In the 1880s, other reformers in Korea also urged the government to adopt a drastic policy to promote industries by introducing advanced machineries and technology from Western countries.

Amid this atmosphere of reform, some new and modern industries emerged around the turn of the twentieth century. The Bank of Chosun (Chosun means Korea), the first modern bank in Korea, was established in 1896. Several other banks followed suit. At the end of 1911, there were 86 factories run by Korean businessmen. Of these factories, 20 were engaged in pottery, 15 in rice processing, 13 in metals, 10 in woven goods, 9 in paper, and 8 in tobacco. Others were engaged in the flour, jewelry, leather, and printing industries (Cho 1974).

Despite the harsh restrictions under Japanese colonialism, several Korean nationalistic entrepreneurs still emerged. They urged the Koreans to educate themselves and to build their own industries. Kim Sung Soo and Lee Sung Hun are two good examples of these patriotic businessmen (Cho 1974). Kim, a son of a wealthy landlord, established Kyung Sung Textile Co., Ltd. in 1919, one of the largest Korean enterprises at that time. In addition to this enterprise, in 1920, Kim also founded the *Dong-A Daily News,* a daily newspaper to provide news to the Korean people. Kim then took over Bosung College (now Korea University) which had financial troubles. Kim was actually a nationalistic pioneering entrepreneur in that he was preoccupied by the restoration of national independence of Korea from Japan. Kim believed that the shortcut to this goal was to develop industries and to promote education for Koreans by Koreans.

Lee Sung Hun (Cho 1974) started his career as an entrepreneur and ended it as an educator. He established a brassware factory in 1887 and became a successful businessman. However, he gradually changed into a nationalistic entrepreneur and established Osan School in 1907 to provide an opportunity for education to many young Koreans. The following year, Lee established both the Taegook Book Store and the Pottery Manufacturing Company. Throughout his career, Lee was preoccupied with the restoration of Korea's independence.

Under colonial rule, the Japanese authorities pursued their own self-interests and forced the Koreans to submit to their demands. Accordingly, Koreans were unable to initiate any venture independently. However, some businessmen were very successful in their ventures because they had learned to balance skillfully between their own interests and those of the Japanese authorities.

After the Japanese defeat in World War II, the Koreans again tried to manage their own economy, but the devastation due to the colonial exploitation of the Japanese and the ensuing Korean Conflict left Koreans heavily dependent on foreign aid. The United States provided more than three billion dollars to South Korea until the U.S. government terminated the aid program in the early 1960s (Krueger 1979). This aid program, however, had become a major source of capital formation in South Korea.

After the Korean Conflict and with American aid, South Korean businessmen began to produce plate glass, fertilizer, and cement. The so-called three "white" industries (sugar refineries, flour mills, and textile mills) flourished in South Korea with the raw materials supplied by the United States. The U.S. assistance program aimed mostly at rebuilding the consumer goods industry and paid little attention to heavy industry in South Korea. Thus, this policy led to an unbalanced economy, which persisted until the first part of the 1960s. Another source of capital was the acquisition of the Japanese property left in South Korea. The Koreans used some of this property to start their own businesses.

There was a close relationship between the South Korean government and businessmen in the distribution of the Japanese property in South Korea and the American aid. Some of the Korean businessmen and nonbusinessmen were successful in participating in the disposal of the Japanese property in South Korea and the American aid. All of these Koreans had close relationships with government officials who had influence over the process of disposing of the property as well as over the funds and materials from the United States. On many occasions, a quid pro quo existed between the government officials and businessmen. During this reconstruction period, some of the businessmen became successful; later in the 1960s and 1970s, they became founders of powerful chaebol groups. In one sense, Korean businessmen have always been political businessmen, because they are a hybrid of government and business. Only those with close ties to the government could be successful. We call this phenomenon the "Principle of Government Business Tie-up."

However, this government-business relationship was not reciprocal. The government leaders exercised great control of the economy, but the businessmen had little impact on politics. This phenomenon is still true today. Traditionally, Koreans have observed a culture based on the mentality "government officials first, and the civilians last." The Korean expression "kwanjon minbee" means, respect the government officials and do not respect the civilians. The South Korean government has had undisputed authority over business. We call this phenomenon the "Principle of Government Supremacy."

Chung Ju Yung, the founder of the $50 billion Hyundai Group, has changed this tradition in South Korea by forming the United People's Party, which won 10 percent of the General Assembly seats or 32 seats (Nakarmi 1992). This is the reverse trend of the Government Supremacy

Principle in that businessmen are beginning to have critical impact on the government. However, one line should be drawn clearly in order to understand this new trend. Chung became a politician after he resigned from the honorary chairmanship of his powerful chaebol group. This signifies that technically, he is a politician and not a businessman, even though Chung was criticized for informally using the chaebol's funds and personnel for his political ambition. It remains to be seen whether this deviation from tradition will become a norm in the South Korean society.

The government's supremacy was particularly evident in the decades of the 1960s through the 1980s when the government implemented the successive five-year economic plans that produced the so-called "miracle of Han River." Koreans call it "Guided Capitalism," (Lim 1975) or "South Korea, Inc." Both titles refer to the government's central role in initiating the five-year economic plans and in intervening in the economy to implement them. Nevertheless, the Korean government disregarded strong criticism concerning the government economic policy from some sectors of society and pursued its own course.

In the early 1960s, the government launched a new progressive economic policy to eliminate hunger and poverty from society by establishing the first five-year economic plan for the 1962–1966 period. Encouraged by the success of the first plan, the government has continuously formulated and successfully implemented new five-year economic plans ever since. Presently, South Korea is in the seventh economic plan (1992–1996).

The economic growth rates under the five-year economic plans as shown in Table 3.1 have been very impressive. Economic growth rates of both 1986 and 1987 were impressively high: 12.5 percent and 12.2 percent, respectively. The growth rates of 1990 and 1991 were also impressive: 9.3 percent, and 8.4 percent, respectively. The South Korean economy has grown significantly despite the political turmoil, labor strife, and student riots.

The goals of the first through the seventh five-year economic plans are listed below: The goal of the first five-year economic plan was to lay a foundation for future economic growth by developing the base industry in South Korea. The second five-year plan implemented the strategy to expand exports and to develop import substitutes through extensive foreign capital. The synthetic fiber, petrochemical, and electronic appliance industries led in the economic growth under this five-year plan. The third five-year economic plan was designed to promote petrochemical, steel, and shipbuilding as exporting industries and to foster the production of electronics and motor vehicles as potential export items. In 1975, 12 firms were licensed as trading companies to promote the export of South Korean goods to overseas markets.

Table 3.1
Five-Year Economic Plans

Five-year Economic Plans	GNP Growth Rate
The first five-year (1962-1966) plan	7.8%
The second five-year (1967-1971) plan	9.6
The third five-year (1972-1976) plan	9.7
The fourth five-year (1977-1981) plan	5.8
The fifth five-year (1982-1986) plan	8.6
The sixth five-year (1987-1991) plan	9.9
The seventh five-year (1992-1996) plan	7.5*

Source: Economic Planning Board, Korea Statistical Yearbook, 1992.
*Estimated real average growth

The goal of the fourth five-year economic plan was to continue to develop heavy industry and to improve the chronic trade imbalance. The fifth five-year plan also emphasized exporting and increasing the competitiveness of heavy industry. The goal of the sixth five-year plan was to achieve optimal growth and equitable distribution of national income. Another important goal was to reduce significantly the amount of foreign debt by increasing exports. Finally, the goal of the seventh five-year plan is to maintain the balance between growth and stability. Another major goal of the plan is to achieve more equitable economy by regulating the economic concentration of the chaebol groups.

In order to achieve the goal of rapid economic growth, the South Korean government has adopted a policy of concentrating wealth in the hands of a few capable businessmen in order to accelerate the saving and investment sequence. No one can deny the contribution made by these businessmen to the phenomenal economic growth of South Korea since the 1960s. South Koreans owe them, in part, for their economic growth. In 1961, the GNP per capita was $82, one of the lowest in the world; by 1991, this figure increased to $6,498 (The Bank of Korea 1992).

This policy of concentrating capital in the hands of a few businessmen, however, also resulted in producing a few wealthy and powerful chaebol groups in South Korea during the last thirty years. This further polarized the unequal distribution of income among the Korean people. According to the Economic Planning Board, while the upper 20 percent of the income class possess 39.6 percent of the nation's wealth, the lower 40 percent of the income class possesses only 21 percent. A huge concentration of the wealth among a few chaebol groups was the major cause of social unrest among students and workers in the 1970s and 1980s. This policy contrasts sharply with the policy of the Taiwan government.

Mostly small and medium-sized companies produced the economic growth in Taiwan. This phenomenon resulted in a rather equal distribution of the nation's wealth.

Another important policy of the South Korean government has been to encourage the use of foreign loans to fuel economic development by insisting that liability is an asset. This massive inflow of foreign capital, sometimes with high interest rates, has become a source of funds for many business corporations in a country where there had never been enough domestic capital formation for economic growth. According to the Bank of Korea (1992), total foreign loans amounted to $40.18 billion at the end of February 1992. This policy also differs from the policy of the Taiwan government, which has emphasized loan-free economic growth. There is no outstanding loan in Taiwan.

Despite its precarious political environment, South Korea has not only survived but actually succeeded because of the ability of its people to adapt to such adversities. In 1968, the South Korean government decided to participate in the Vietnam War by sending troops there. Businessmen rallied around the flag of Korean soldiers. Some ventured into international business, and one of them was fortunate enough to become a founder of a chaebol group. Cho Choong Honn, the chairman of Hanjin Group, accumulated his fortune by transporting supplies for both the American and South Korean armies at great risk to his own life in the midst of the Vietnam War. Hyundai Group, founded by Chung Ju Yung, also expanded its business significantly by engaging in business during the Vietnam War.

South Koreans particularly felt the impact of oil shock in the early 1970s because they depended almost completely on foreign oil for their energy consumption. To overcome this crisis, the South Korean government initiated various economic projects to improve relations with the Middle East countries, notably Saudi Arabia. South Korean businessmen competed with those from other developed countries and won many projects in Saudi Arabia and its oil-rich neighbors. The industrious work of South Koreans impressed the host countries, and participating companies from South Korea earned huge profits from these projects. Thus, South Koreans intelligently overcame the oil crisis.

The phenomenal growth of the South Korean economy since the early 1960s was the result of the joint effort of the government and business. The government planned for the economy, and businessmen implemented these plans in their enterprises. Again, there was a strong tie-up relationship between the government and business. The government played an unmistakably powerful role in shaping the economy and guiding businessmen in accordance with the economic plans. The government provided various economic incentives to some businessmen, such as very low interest loans and the rights to take over some business ventures.

Of course, a give and take situation existed. First of all, these businessmen were expected to support government policies, both political and economic, to receive such favoritism. They were also implicitly required to return some of their profits to political leaders through contributions. Chung Ju Yung claimed that he donated 10 billion won (close to $13 million at the exchange rate of $1 to 770 won) in one year to the office of the President (Contributed Even 10 Billion Won 1992). In one sense, the contribution was a quasi-tax to businessmen, but in return, government officials guaranteed them their businesses. Many businessmen considered it as a part of operating costs for their businesses. It may not be an exaggeration when we say that the South Korean government created powerful chaebol groups in South Korea. They are indeed the products of the "South Korea, Inc."

The relationship between government and business is a unique feature in the Korean management system in that the government establishes policy guidelines for businesses to follow. In many cases, businesses respond proactively to these guidelines of the government policies for their ventures. The government's leadership is based on the Principle of Government Supremacy: The government is capable of leading businesses. This confidence of the government is again based on the capability of government technocrats. These technocrats belong to an elite; they are graduates of the most prestigious universities in South Korea, and Koreans have a strong trust in them for their capability and leadership. Technocracy is still a highly respected occupation because the impressive economic growth since the 1960s in South Korea is the result of a very productive combination of determined political leadership, capable government technocrats, and proactive businesses.

The merchant class has had a low status in the traditional Korean society. However, Korean leaders understood infallibly that the only way to regain independence from the Japanese colonialism was to improve education and industry. They encouraged businessmen to take the initiative in this endeavor. As a result, many capable businessmen emerged in a land where business had never been encouraged.

In the early 1960s, the government also appealed to businessmen to initiate enterprises to solve the age-old problem of the absolute poverty of the Korean people. Korean businessmen responded positively to this call for the country and for their own interests. Some of the businessmen were very successful through tactical tie-up with the government; others were successful with their own entrepreneurial talents without extensive tie-up with the government. Without these entrepreneurial spirits to challenge the unknown world, the South Korean economy would never have been taken off the ground. Of course, not all of the businessmen succeeded in their ventures; there have been many failures. However, there appeared to be more successes in risk-taking ventures in South Korea than failures.

In the next chapter, we will discuss entrepreneurs in Korea before 1945 and in South Korea after the end of World War II. Without them, it is almost futile to discuss the Korean management system. By their unique leadership and management style, these entrepreneurs have formed the unique management system in South Korea.

REFERENCES

The Bank of Korea. *The Preliminary Statistics of the Economy of 1991*. Seoul: The Bank of Korea, 1992.

Cho, K. J. *Hankuk Kiupkasa* (History of Korean Entrepreneurs). 2d ed. Seoul: Parkyongsa, 1974.

Contributed Even 10 Billion Won as a Political Contribution. *The Dong-A Daily News* (January 9, 1992).

Korean Overseas Information Service. *A Handbook of Korea*. 3d ed. Seoul: Korean Information Service, Ministry of Culture and Information, 1979.

Krueger, A. O. *The Development Role of the Foreign Sector and Aid*. Cambridge, Mass.: Council on East Asia Studies, Harvard University, 1979.

Lim, C. C. Industry Development of South Korea since World War II. *The Discourse of Economics* 14(2). Seoul National University, 1975.

Nakarmi, L. A Chaebol Plays Hardball with Roh Tae Woo. *Business Week* (February 24, 1992).

4

Entrepreneurs in Korea (until 1945) and South Korea (after 1945)

ENTREPRENEURS BEFORE 1945

Without ventures by entrepreneurs, there would be no management system. Korean entrepreneurs initiated many ventures and developed a unique Korean management system. To understand this system, it is important first to review the historical trend of entrepreneurs in Korea (South Korea after World War II). This historical review encompasses four periods: the enlightenment or awakening (1876–1910), the Japanese occupation (1910–1945), the instability and reconstruction (1945–1962), and the period of rapid growth and expansion (1962–present).

Not surprisingly, the early entrepreneurs engaged mostly in light industries, particularly textiles. Ahn Hyeong Su established the Daehan Weaving Shop in 1897 with a strong endorsement from the government. In addition, Min Beong Suk and Kim Duck Chang started the Chongro Weaving Shop in 1899 and the Kim Duck Chang Weaving Shop in 1902, respectively. Unlike other shop owners, Kim operated his shop with Western machines (Cho 1974).

In 1898, Park Chong Gee founded the Buha Railroad Company with his own capital and installed a 6-kilometer (3.7 miles) railway system between Hatahn and Pusan. However, his business collapsed when the Japanese built a railroad system between Seoul and Pusan in 1899. In 1896, Kim Chong Han and nine others established the Chosun Bank, the first modern banking system in Korea. The Han Sung Bank and the Daehan Chunil Bank were established shortly afterwards in 1897 and 1903, respectively (Cho 1974).

Several wealthy merchants started textile mills in 1890 and 1910 during the period when Korea was annexed by Japan. Among them, Paek Yun

Su, Kim Yun Myun, and Park Sung Jik were outstanding businessmen. Paek inherited his family's silk fabric business and expanded it despite the environment of Japanese control. He also established Taechang Trading Co., Ltd. with a capital of 500,000 won and expanded it into a modernized (or Westernized) corporation. This is the origin of the contemporary Taechang Group. Kim Yun Myun engaged in cotton cloth manufacturing in 1919 and was a founding member of the Dongyang Products Company with a capital of 2 million won. Park Sung Jik began his cotton cloth production in 1898. In 1905, Park and a Japanese businessman established the Kongiksa Company, whose capital expanded to one million won in 1921. He also invested in other companies. This is the origin of the present-day Doosan Group (Cho 1974).

Some Korean businessmen operated book stores which numbered more than twenty around the turn of the century. Others engaged in publishing and printing shops contributed significantly to the modernization of Korea by publishing and selling books (Cho 1974).

Modern department stores also emerged. Dong-A Department Store and Hwashin Department Store were the big stores in Korea. Choi Nam opened the four-story Dong-A Department Store in 1931 in downtown Seoul which employed approximately 200 employees and was the first department store in Korea. Several years later, however, the Hwashin Department Store, owned by Park Heung Sik, absorbed his store. In 1937, Park opened the largest department store in Korea at that time. He also introduced the chain store concept from Western countries and applied it by establishing more than 300 chain stores throughout Korea. Park was one of the most successful businessmen in Korea for almost four decades (Cho 1974).

Several businessmen in the region of Kaesong rose to such prominence that they were collectively called "the Kaesong merchants." Kaesong is located just north of the armistice line of the Korean Conflict and was known for the cultivation of ginseng. Son Bong Jo and other businessmen started the Yungshin Joint-Stock Company in 1912 with a capital of 300,000 won, the business line of which was wholesaling and retailing, warehousing, and financing. In 1913, another firm, Kaesongsa, similar to the Yungshin Company, was established principally by Choi Kee Chang with a capital of 50,000 won. In 1917, Kong Seong Hak and his associates invested 50,000 won to begin the Kaesong Electric Company, which introduced electricity to that region (Cho 1974).

The region of Pyongyang (now the capital city of North Korea) was the center of the Korean rubber shoe and hosiery industries. Lee Byung Du was a pioneering entrepreneur who, around 1919, built a rubber shoe factory in Pyongyang with four other businessmen. Lee designed shoes for males and females because the so-called Korean rubber shoes satisfied the traditional taste of Koreans. The business grew briskly and increased in profits and capacity and was one of a few industries that Korean businessmen dominated under the Japanese occupation. Most of the entrepreneurs in this industry in this region were dedicated Christians (Cho 1974) who, before World War II, called Pyongyang "another Jerusalem." It is ironic that "another Jerusalem" has become the capital city of North Korea, a stubborn Communist country.

The hosiery industry was developed in the Pyongyang area, with most of the venture starting on a small scale. Kim Kee Ho started his hosiery business in 1906 by installing four weaving machines imported from Japan. Lee Jin Soon, Noh Duck Kyu, Park Chi Rok, Son Chang Yun, Oh Kyung Suk, and Bang Yun were also pioneering entrepreneurs in this industry. Most of these businessmen operating in the region of North Korea fled to the South when the Communists took over North Korea after World War II and rebuilt their businesses in South Korea where some of them have become prominent businessmen.

Bang Ui Suck was another entrepreneur who dominated the transportation industry in the northeastern region of Korea. Bang became the president of Kong Heung Transportation Company at the age of 31. He expanded the business by using his entrepreneurial talent and also established Ham Heung Taxi Company in 1929, Bukseon Transportation Company in 1932, and Cheil Taxi Company in 1936. In 1940, Bang consolidated these existing companies into one giant company, completing the monopoly of transportation in the northeastern region of Korea by acquiring two other transportation companies. He also participated by his investments in other fields, such as warehousing, the brewing industry, the lumber industry, fisheries, and electricity (Cho 1974).

These are examples of successful entrepreneurs before the end of World War II. Some of them continued their businesses after World War II in South Korea.

ENTREPRENEURS AFTER WORLD WAR II

After the war, there emerged another group of entrepreneurs who are still actively involved in their businesses. In this group, Chung Ju Yung is a typical entrepreneur (Chung 1991). He is the founder of Hyundai Group and is the twelfth most wealthy person in the world according to *Fortune* magazine (Losee 1992). Chung was born to a very poor farm family and had only a sixth grade education. In January 1950, Chung established a small car repair shop. The Korean Conflict of June 1950 provided him with an opportunity to use his genius in business and he was successful in bidding on a public works contract to build new facilities for war efforts. After the war, Chung (Choi 1982) actively participated in the bidding to rebuild many facilities damaged during the war. The contracts bidding to rebuild the Han River bridge in 1957 and the multipurpose dam of Soyang River in 1967 laid a solid foundation for his business to grow into one the largest chaebol groups in South Korea. Chung demonstrated his entrepreneurial talent during and after the Korean Conflict.

The South Korean government called for the bidding on these projects, and Chung's company became a contractor ad libitum in most cases. Chung's company and government officials frequently developed a close relationship. If the government had not awarded his company with such great opportunities, Chung might not have become a giant in business, and his empire of Hyundai Group would not exist today. The government treated Chung preferentially mainly because he had two unique capacities as a businessman. He was—and still is—a man of vision, determination, action, and sometimes foolhardiness. He also was able to obtain political favors from politicians and high ranking government officials.

During the aftermath of the 1973 oil embargo, Chung extended his vision to the Middle East countries and to Saudi Arabia in particular. He succeeded in bidding for projects in Saudi Arabia and in other countries in the region, and he demonstrated to the world the superiority of the Korean engineering capability and the effective performance of the Korean manpower.

Chung decided to establish a comprehensive motor vehicle plant with a capacity to produce 80,000 units in 1973 when there was a demand of only 7,000 units of cars in South Korea. He also manufactured many important parts for motor vehicles. The first Pony cars were produced in December 1975, and many Koreans criticized his venture as too risky and ambitious. However, Chung persevered. It is a well-known fact that Hyundai Excel cars were first exported to Canada in 1983 and became the top import car that year. He then extended the capacity of the factory to 450,000 units in 1985 and started to export the cars to the United States in 1986.

Chung also established a shipyard of one million-ton capacity in 1970, the largest in the world at that time. No one knew whether or not the shipyard would receive any orders from foreign shipping companies because these companies did not have any information concerning the Korean shipbuilding capacity. However, Chung insisted on the shipyard saying, "A ship is nothing but an engine surrounded by iron plates." The shipyard was completed in 27 months, the world's shortest construction time, and received an order for a 260,000 ton tanker while the shipyard was still under construction (Choi 1982).

Daewoo Group was initially established by Kim Woo Choong in 1967, when he was 31 years old (Choi 1982). While he was working as an employee for a company, Kim realized his entrepreneurial talents and used this capacity fully by establishing a textile mill. Kim envisioned the implementation of import quotas for textile goods by the United Stated in advance. Before the quota system was implemented, Kim exported an ambitiously large volume of textile goods to the United States and was allocated the largest quota, surpassing the big textile companies in Japan, Taiwan, and Hong Kong.

Kim's entrepreneurial talents include vision, determination, stamina, and tireless energy. He travels abroad several times a year to supervise and negotiate worldwide projects and is said to sleep only four hours a night. Kim was also very fortunate to have received political favors from the late President Park Chung Hee, who knew that Kim was a son of his beloved teacher. Because of this relationship, President Park provided preferential treatment to Kim such as low interest loans.

Kim has another advantage. Since he was a graduate of prestigious schools, Kyunggi High School and Yonsei University, he can obtain political and financial support from alumni of both schools, who dominate the government and the financial world. He has also been able to recruit capable graduates from these schools as employees and managers for his corporations (Oh 1986).

The late Lee Byung Chull (Lee 1986), the founder of Samsung Group, made a fortune by building a sugar refinery right after the Korean Conflict (Choi 1982). This fortune laid the solid foundation for Samsung Group as he expanded his business into many other areas. Lee insisted that his companies be the largest and the best in South Korea and in Asia. When he built the Silla Hotel in Seoul, he was determined to build the largest and the best in South Korea. Later he was bitterly disappointed to learn that the Lotte Hotel, which was built almost simultaneously by another company in Seoul, was a superior facility. He further demonstrated his resolve by building a bigger golf course than the largest one in Japan.

Like other great entrepreneurs in South Korea, Lee (Lee 1986) was a man of vision, action, and politics. In 1968, he wrote an article on the future of the electronics industry for a Korean newspaper in which he described a bright prospect for the industry. After the article was published, his company began to produce electronic products. Samsung has been exporting these products worldwide ever since.

When stocks in the government-owned Heungup Bank were publicly auctioned in 1957, Lee became the third highest bidder. However, it turned out that Lee succeeded in taking over 85 percent of shares by playing politics. This is a typical example of a relationship between the government and business. He was successful in politicking for his business and also took over 50 percent of the Chohung Bank shares and 30 percent of the Commercial Bank shares. He was, therefore, able to influence the operation of commercial banks in South Korea. Lee was accused of being a corrupt businessman whenever the government changed hands, but he always escaped prosecution and prospered.

One of Lee's best contributions was the effective training of managers in his organizations. Koreans regard his corporations as "the military academy of management." This phrase implies that capable managers are trained under his leadership and management philosophy. Evaluation based solely on performance was his basic management philosophy and he promoted and demoted his subordinates strictly on this basis.

The late Koo In Hwoi, founder of Lucky–Goldstar Group, began his business in 1940 by establishing "Kooin Shop" (Choi 1982). He was very fortunate to meet the right people at the right times. For example, he met Hur Man Jong and his son, Hur Joon Koo, right after he failed in his trading venture with Japan in 1945. The senior Hur offered to help Koo by investing one-fourth of the needed capital in Koo's trading company, marking the beginning of a close relationship between the Koo and Hur families in Lucky–Goldstar Group.

In 1946, Koo met another important businessman, Kim Hak Jun, an expert on cosmetic creams in South Korea. Koo and Kim established the Lucky Chemical Industrial Company, Ltd. to manufacture cosmetic creams. The demand for their products was so brisk that the company made a fortune, which became the foundation of Lucky–Goldstar Group. He named his company Lucky, after Lucky Strike, a popular American cigarette brand in South Korea at that time.

The company then produced plastic containers for creams with U.S. imported machinery. In 1954, the company began to produce Lucky toothpaste, the company's main brand, in addition to toothbrushes, combs, and soap containers. In 1959, Koo established another company, "Kumsungsa" (the Goldstar Company), which produced radio sets. Koo called his combined company, "Lucky–Goldstar," and it was the first South Korean company to establish an assembly plant in the United States. A plant was built in Huntsville, Alabama, in 1982 to produce television sets.

Koo and his top executives demonstrated their skills in politicking when they waged an aggressive four-year campaign against Daehan Electric Company in order to dominate the electric cable industry in the domestic market. The Koo group won this so-called war with government assistance. Lucky–Goldstar Group absorbed Daehan, which now operates under the name of Goldstar Electric Company. A close relationship with the government also played a crucial role when Lucky–Goldstar Group bought out the government-run Honam Oil Refinery.

Lim Dai Hong is a rather unique entrepreneur in South Korea in that he has been developing commercial items through his own research activities (Choi 1982). His Miwon Group corporations manufacture more than 30 products, all of which were developed by Lim himself. He has one research laboratory in his office and has another in his home, where he spends much of his time. People call him an "experimental maniac." The Japanese demanded 100 million yen to provide Lim with the technical know-how of producing the major Miwon product, monosodium glutamate. Instead of paying such a huge sum, he spent day and night for almost one hundred days in developing his own process for producing it.

Lim is also a unique entrepreneur in South Korea because he has never sought political favors for his business. He has no close relationship with the government, a rare case in the climate of South Korea. His business has experienced tremendous disadvantages because of this, but he has insisted on the separation of business and politics. Nevertheless, his business has been prosperous.

Cho Choong Honn, the founder of Hanjin Group, previously was mentioned briefly (Choi 1982). He started his transportation business with one used truck after World War II but accumulated a fortune by becoming a trustworthy supplier of goods to the U.S. Army stationed in South Korea. This business increased from $70,000 to $1,300,000 in just two years, earning his reputation with honest business dealings. For instance, one of his truck drivers sold 1,200 U.S. Army parkas, worth $30,000, to merchants in the market. Cho bought back these uniforms by visiting individual merchants and returned them to the U.S. Army in South Korea.

Cho also laid a foundation for his Hanjin Group by using his visionary insights. In 1965, while visiting Vietnam with some South Korean government officials, he foresaw a tremendous opportunity for his business. With the help of his younger brother, Cho Choong Kun, a graduate of the University of California, he approached the Pentagon in Washington, D.C. to obtain permission to operate a freight venture in Vietnam. Friendships with American officers when he was a military supplier to the U.S. Army were helpful in the negotiations and after a month of negotiation, the Pentagon gave permission. Through this risky venture in Vietnam, Cho made another fortune.

Cho and his Hanjin Group are well known as owners and operators of Korean Air. On January 21, 1969, when the government-run Industrial Bank announced the public sale of Korean Air, there were no bidders because the required security deposit was 145 million won. No companies were able to raise the necessary cash in such a short time period. After having failed twice to sell the company, the Industrial Bank offered a contract ad libitum to cash-rich Cho. Korean Air is now a thriving company in Hanjin Group.

On February 12, 1987, the government awarded the right to operate a second airline in South Korea to Kumho Group. Anticipating such an award, top-ranking chaebol groups, including Samsung, Lucky–Goldstar, Hyundai, Daewoo, Doosan, and Hankuk Hwayak secretly prepared detailed plans for the bidding. Kumho ranked twentieth among chaebol groups, so it is not clear why the government chose Kumho Group. Some observers speculated about Kumho's relationship with political leaders, but it is difficult to verify this speculation at the time of this writing. Kumho Group's Asiana Airlines has developed domestic routes and has been expanded to include international routes, such as that to the United States.

Kumho Group began its business in 1946 with two taxies run by Park In Chun, an ex-police officer. After failing in all of his other ventures (Choi 1982), Park's company became the largest bus company in South Korea with more than 650 buses. His successful strategy initiated long-distance bus routes, which many bus companies in South Korea were reluctant to implement.

After a slow start, the company quickly expanded. In 1960, Kumho Group established a tire company, followed by a synthetic rubber company in 1970, and a company for exporting tires in 1972. The group took over both Kukdong Steel in 1976, and a textile company in 1977, and has been managed by Park Seong Yong, the eldest son of the founder, who earned his Ph.D. degree in Economics from Yale University and who taught at the University of California, Berkeley, until he returned home in 1968. He then served as a government official and a college professor until he became the chairman of the group when his father passed away.

There are many successful entrepreneurs in South Korea. However, there are also many unsuccessful entrepreneurs. Although most of them have entrepreneurial capacity, they failed in their business for common reasons classified as follows:

- No managerial capacity
- Bad timing
- No show of interest in relationship with influential politicians
- Connections with the wrong politicians
- Wrong product lines or business items
- Unfavorable changes of domestic and international environments
- Combinations of the above

Yang Jung Mo is a typical example of an unsuccessful entrepreneur (Cho 1987). He was the chairman of Kukje Group, an upper-ranking chaebol group in South Korea. Suddenly in February 1985, the government ordered him to dissolve his group. The South Korean government gave no clear explanation for its action. Speculation included two possible reasons for Yang's demise: He refused to have any relationship with powerful political leaders and the timing was not right for him. The financial situation of his group rapidly deteriorated at the time of its dissolution because his exporting business had become stagnant. His group could have survived if they had endured a couple months more because the exporting environment turned around favorably after the group's dissolution. It is ironic that out of 23 corporations he gave up, all but one are operating profitably.

Chung Jae Ho is another such example of an unsuccessful entrepreneur (Cho 1987). In 1966, he had 12 corporations with 12,000 employees. His assets amounted to 10 billion won, his annual sales reached 8 billion won, and his exports amounted to $11 million. This statistic comprised 90 percent of all South Korean exports at that time. He became bankrupt in the 1970s mainly because he was unable to pay his loan from Japan. Right after he obtained this loan however, his burden doubled because of the change in exchange rates. Chung asked for government assistance, but received a cool response because a high ranking government official was hostile toward him.

Kim Chang Won is one of the founding fathers of the South Korean motor vehicle (Cho 1987). In 1964, after taking over the Saenara Motor Company, he began producing the Corona car in association with Toyota of Japan. Demand for the car was brisk, and he quickly made a fortune. However, his misfortune began with the withdrawal of Toyota from South Korea after the announcement of the Four Principles of Chou En-lai of Communist China. Chou's principles prohibited economic cooperation with any country that had business with Taiwan, and South Korea had a close business relation with that country.

After Toyota, Kim negotiated a contract with General Motors of the United States in 1972, but G.M. cars produced in South Korea were not well received by consumers. However, it was speculated that an influential political leader stopped supporting Kim's business. In 1983, Daewoo Group took over G.M. Korea and has been producing Pontiac LeMans, designed by Germany's Opel, for both domestic and overseas markets. Recently Daewoo Group also severed its business relation with General Motors.

These founding entrepreneurs have had a critical impact in forming and implementing the management system in Korea until 1945 and in South Korea after 1945. Their management styles are often unique, but they also share management features that cannot be found in management systems of other nations. These common features are the basic characteristics of the Korean management system, which will be discussed later in this book.

In the next chapter, the behavioral pattern of the Koreans will be discussed. Korean culture, based on the Chinese culture, and the geopolitical environment have had a significant impact on Korean behavioral patterns. In one sense, the Korean management system is a function of the behavioral pattern of its people, signifying that no one can understand the Korean management system unless he or she comprehends the behavioral pattern of the Korean people.

REFERENCES

Cho, K. J. *Hankuk Kiupkasa* (History of Korean Entrepreneurs). Seoul: Parkyungsa, 1974.

Cho, N. J. Manghan Chaebol Chongsudul (Liquidated Chaebol Groups). *The Monthly Chosun* (March, 1987).

Choi, C. L. *Chaebol Eshiposhi* (The 25 Hours of Chaebol). Seoul: The Economic Department of the Chosun Daily News, 1982.

Chung, J. Y. My Enterprise and My Life (in Korean). *The Dong-A Daily News* (July 13-October 11, 1991).

Lee, B. C. *Hoam Jajun* (My Biography). Seoul: The Choong Ang Daily News, 1986.

Losee, S. The Billionaires. *Fortune* (September 7, 1992).

Oh, H. C. Kim Woo Choong: A Commander in Motion (in Korean). *The Monthly Chosun* (September, 1986).

5

Behavioral Patterns of the Koreans

Some Japanese scholars are amazed by the striking differences in behavioral patterns between the Koreans and the Japanese who have both shared the Oriental culture for more than a thousand years. During this time, group behavior is not only a norm but also a virtue. However, the Japanese scholars observed that the Koreans exercised individualistic behavior that cannot be traced in Japan.

Hayashi (1985) stated that the Korean people maintained individualistic behavior different from group-oriented behavior. Hasegawa (1987) also identified a unique individualistic behavior of the Korean people in his book *Challenging Koreans* (in Japanese). Kusayanagi (1980) mentioned that no common features of behavioral patterns existed between the Koreans and the Japanese. He also emphasized that these two societies were based on completely different behavioral patterns; collective group activities in Japan and individualistic behavior in South Korea. Watanabe (1987) recognized different behavioral patterns of the two nations from the standpoint of loyalty and pointed out that the Koreans demonstrated their loyalty to individuals in a group while the Japanese distinguished themselves by showing their loyalty to their group.

Korean scholars also uncovered these same individualistic behavioral patterns in the Koreans. Kim (1982) disclosed an individualistic way of thinking and also observed selfish behavior. Kim and Kim (1989) dealt with individualistic behavior of the Koreans, but Kim (1988) strongly denied individualistic behavioral patterns among them, based on his assertion that the Oriental culture has never nurtured an individualistic behavior. Nevertheless, Kim readily admitted that there existed some traces of individualistic behavior in South Korea, which could not be identified in Japan. Kim defended his seemingly conflicting claim by emphasizing that individualistic behavior within the Koreans was a peripheral phenomenon in a group-oriented society. Chang (1989), a Korean-American scholar, also found an individualistic behavior pattern among Korean people, and he discussed this behavior in the context of geopolitical and sociocultural environments.

Lee (1977) emphasized a strong group consciousness of the Korean people at both the family and community levels. However, he also mentioned their individualistic behavior. Cha (1988) edited the research outcomes of the Korean Economic Research Center of the Korean Chamber of Commerce. An outcome of the research is that while senior and experienced managers are engaged in group activities, young, new managers and employees are more interested in individualistic behavior. The research implies that generational differences can explain the behavioral pattern of the Koreans.

The individualistic behavioral pattern of the Koreans, of course, is clearly different from that of Americans, which is based on Jeffersonian individualism. Americans pursue individualism outside of the context of the group. As a result, individual activities and group activities are easily separable in this situation. Koreans, on the other hand, pursue individualistic aspirations within the context of a group, and their individualistic behavior often cannot be separated from the group behavior.

The purpose of this chapter is to distinguish behavioral patterns of the Korean people in the context of individualistic and group behavior that have an impact on management in both business and other organizations in South Korea. We will apply concepts such as the Salad Bowl Group (as opposed to the Melting Pot Group), Trust-Base Scale, I-We Consciousness Grid, and the Informality of Group, to the understanding of behavioral patterns of the Korean people. Although we can apply this study to the people in North Korea, we exclude them from this chapter.

The assumptions of this study are as follows:

1. The Korean people have developed a concurrent behavioral pattern of individualistic and group activity. They therefore experience conflict when they pursue their individualistic interests, but they must also compromise themselves in order to accomplish group interests. Concepts as the I-We Consciousness Grid and Salad Bowl Group are relevant to the verification process of this assumption.

2. The Korean people often have a tendency to pursue their individualistic aspirations through informal groups. This signifies that they have a tendency to organize informal groups and transform formal groups into quasi-informal groups. We call this tendency "an informality of formal groups." The four concepts mentioned above verify this assumption.

3. The Korean people clearly identify who are their friends and who are not. They trust their friends and coax them into their informal groups in order to

facilitate their own or common interests. They ignore those Koreans who are not their friends and often display a sense of hostility toward them. The Trust-Base Scale is specifically relevant for verifying this assumption.

SALAD BOWL GROUP VERSUS MELTING POT GROUP

Kumon (1980), a Japanese scholar, cites the combination of oxygen and hydrogen to exemplify the different behavioral patterns between the Japanese and the Koreans. According to Kumon, the Koreans remain as molecules of oxygen and hydrogen without undergoing a chemical change into water. Some of them might be transformed into water, but the majority of them remain as independent and separable molecules. We will call this phenomenon the "Salad Bowl Group."

In this case, the "I" feeling coexists with the "We" feeling in a group. The "I" feeling signifies the independent and individualistic interests in a group, while the "We" feeling means a group consciousness, group cohesiveness, and group loyalty. The "I" feeling usually is a dominant form in a group setting in South Korea. On many occasions, when these two feelings are mutually exclusive, a sense of conflict develops in the minds of those involved in this situation. As a result, the behavior of the group members is very volatile and unpredictable by nature. Teamwork is weak, and hot arguments persist. The only outcome of this situation is violent confrontation, factiousness, and a lack of compromise. Even if compromises are reached, sometimes they elicit cries of treachery and betrayal among the group members.

However, these feelings can be stabilized if a compromising zone is found, and a group can be productive if any super goals, such as winning a war, are identified and satisfy both individualistic and group interests. This indicates that a Salad Bowl group can go in either a destructive or constructive direction depending on a compromise zone or accepted super goals.

Kumon (1980) further uses the oxygen-hydrogen example to identify a unique behavioral pattern of the Japanese. In this case, he identifies water alone, and it is a meaningless effort to trace molecules of oxygen and hydrogen in water. There are no separate and independent molecules of oxygen and hydrogen in water. We call this phenomenon the "Melting Pot Group." Each member of this group loses his or her own identity and behaves purely as a group member. Only the "We" feeling exists in the group (Murayama 1973), and the "I" feeling is sublimated into the "We" feeling. The identity of each group member is never disclosed. This group behaves purely as a stable, predictable group.

This chapter will focus on the Salad Bowl Group since the major interest of this study is to identify and explain behavioral patterns of the

Figure 5.1
I-We Consciousness Grid

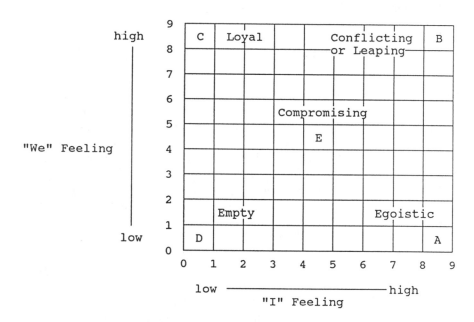

Korean people, and the concept of the Salad Bowl Group alone seems to be relevant. We will apply the concept of the Melting Pot Group only when we need to show the contrast between these two group behaviors.

I-WE CONSCIOUSNESS GRID

The concept of the Salad Bowl Group directly relates to the concept of the I-We Consciousness Grid. Both the ordinate and abscissa of the grid are divided by nine, as shown in Figure 5.1. The ordinate represents the "We" feeling, and the abscissa represents the "I" feeling.

In each corner of the grid is a cell, labeled A to D. Cell A can be called "Egoistic" simply because only selfish or individualistic interests prevail in a group environment, and the sense of group loyalty is absent among members of the group. On the other hand, Cell C can be called "Loyal" because high group consciousness is dominant, and each member is ready to sacrifice individualistic interests to attain group interests.

Cell B can be called "Confronting," or "Leaping" because it is impossible to coexist with both high individualistic aspirations and high group interests. Only an extensive confrontation among members and leaders of a group exists. However, it can be very productive or "Leaping" if the leader of a group is able to identify a super goal that can satisfy both individualistic and group interests.

Cell D can be called "Empty" because both individualistic and group interests are very low. This may be the case of an inactive or a dying group. In the center of the grid is Cell E, which can be called "Compromising" simply because it is at the midpoint of individualistic and group interests. This compromise can be reached easily if the survival of any group is at stake, and every member senses a crisis.

Safire (1987) states that the Koreans were culturally confrontational, and Darlin (1987) mentions that teamwork in South Korea, unlike Japan, was weak. Company loyalty of workers was less than their Japanese counterparts, and job hopping prevailed whenever a better opportunity came along. Bruma (1988) characterizes the factiousness and lack of compromise in South Korea. All of these assertions claim that the Koreans have developed a unique behavioral pattern of individualistic behavior within a group context. The conceptual framework of the Salad Bowl Group and the I-We Consciousness Grid are useful tools to explain the behavior of the South Koreans.

INFORMALITY OF FORMAL GROUPS

Informality of groups is another process of pursuing individualistic interests in a group setting. As mentioned before, the Koreans pursue their individualistic interests in the context of a group, and this seems to be a unique practice. Both informal groups and informality of formal groups are a sure way to accomplish individualistic aspirations in such an environment. Many informal groups are organized on the basis of a Trust-Base Scale, which we will discuss in the following section.

A "gyeh" is a good example of an informal group or an informality of a formal group. A "gyeh" (Money Pools 1986) is an informal group in which group members pool their money to form something much like a credit union, but without a written contract. Each month, a member collects the pooled money from the other members of the "gyeh" until all of the members have that opportunity. Then the group dissolves itself or starts a new "gyeh." The main purpose of this group is to use an informal group to provide individualistic interests in the form of a huge sum of money.

Each member of this "gyeh" organization is carefully screened because each of them must be trusted in the sense that he or she is obliged to contribute the agreed sum of money each month until the last meeting when the last member collects the sum of money for that month. Anyone who does not have the trust-base of the leader or initiator of this "gyeh" group is not allowed to be a member. This "gyeh" group, therefore, is based on mutual trust. The extent of trust is based on the Trust-Base Scale, which will be discussed in detail in this chapter.

Sometimes it is hard to distinguish the informality of formal groups from formal groups. We intend to distinguish them on the basis of individualistic interests. If some or all of the members pursue their individualistic interests by using the benefits or advantages of a group, they use the informality of a formal group. In one sense, any formal organization can be called an informality of a group, because no member abandons his or her individualistic interests completely to pursue group interests only. However, in informal group or informality of a formal group, individualistic interests far outweigh those of formal groups, and some or all of the members use the advantages of groups to accomplish their individualistic interests in a group setting.

A formal group and informality of a formal group are different. A formal group is organized by shared interests, whereas an informality of a formal group has a tendency to transform a formal group into an informality of a formal organization on the basis of the Trust-Base Scale. Of course, informal subgroups exist in a formal group based on pre-established criteria of common interests. However, in an informality of a formal group, all the members in the group almost without exception become members of an informal group based on the Trust-Base Scale.

One of the characteristics of an informality of a formal group is strong personal loyalty of members toward their leader. This person may be the leader of an informal group within a formal group or the leader of an entire group. Each member demonstrates his or her personal loyalty to the leader of an informal group in order to attain maximum benefits of his or her individualistic interests. The leader, in turn, exercises his or her authority to guarantee such aspirations of each member of the group. Therefore, the concept of reciprocity (Chang 1989) plays an important role here, and the political parties in South Korea follow this pattern literally. An indisputable personal loyalty exists to the boss of the group rather than to the group itself. The leader then infallibly takes care of his followers. One newspaper (A President Committed 1992) reported that the president of a small company committed suicide simply because he was unable to pay the wages of his twenty or more employees for three months. As a leader, he was unable to fulfill his obligation to his subordinates. In this extremely rare case, the tragic behavior should be understood from a context of mutual reciprocity between a superior and his subordinates.

From these examples, you can see very powerful but loosely organized groups in South Korea, such as the organization of school classmates and the alumni associations of various schools from elementary school to graduate school. There even exists alumni organizations for Korean students who attended universities in other countries. Organizations of people from the same region, organizations of people with the same family name, organizations of people with the same hobbies, organizations of released political prisoners, and organizations of veterans are a few examples of informal groups or an informality of formal groups in South Korea.

TRUST-BASE SCALE

The Korean people have developed a behavioral pattern of vigorously pursuing individualistic interests through a group setting, and there are numerous such groups in South Korea through which members take advantage of groups for their individualistic interests. The Koreans form informal groups and an informality of formal groups on the basis of the Trust-Base Scale which is defined as the extent of trust one extends toward other people. The Koreans have established and accept a common denominator to the extent of mutual trust culturally and traditionally which they accept. We have developed a Trust-Base Scale which ranges from 1 to 100 as in Table 5.1.

Table 5.1
Trust-Base Scale

Subjects	Trust-Base Scale
Spouse	100
Parents	100
Children	100
Brothers/sisters	100
Nephews/nieces	99
Cousins	97
Relatives	96
Classmates of high school	97
Classmates of college	85
Classmates of elementary school	50
Alumni of high school and college	80
People with the same family name	70
People from the same region	70
People from the different regions	60
People in the same job organization	90
People of the same profession	80
People with the same hobbies	70
Neighbors	70
Same church members	95
People in the same denomination	80
People in different denominations	70
People of different religions	40
Strangers (Koreans)	5
Foreigners (without any relations)	1

The selection criterion for the subjects is based on the FAR concept (Chang 1988) and exclusionism (Kim and Kim 1989). FAR is the acronym for family, alumni, and regionalism in South Korea. Family denotes the family system and its relative importance in the Korean society, alumni signifies the attitude toward education in general and the relative importance of the schools one attended, and regionalism identifies the relative importance of regional sectionalism in the society. Exclusionism recognizes the extent of rejection of strangers and outsiders in the society who are Koreans as well and foreigners and do not have any direct or indirect relation with other Koreans.

The Koreans are one of the most family-centered people in the world, the family system being extremely important. The Koreans exist in order to enhance their family prestige and pride. It is, therefore, an unforgivable shame for anyone to disgrace his or her family pride. Individuals are highly motivated to strive for personal career success in order to upgrade the prestige of their family. Big enterprises in South Korea, such as the chaebol are, in one sense, family enterprises in which the father, sons, sons-in-law, nephews, cousins, and other close relatives play a decisive role in managing their enterprises. As a result, the Trust-Base Scale of family members is close to 100.

The school attended in South Korea is also critically important and friendship with fellow students develops in South Korea just as in other countries. However, the ties of friendship are extremely strong with fellow students in South Korea. A student's future career and even personal life after graduation are influenced greatly by these relationships with fellow alumni. The Koreans who attend the same school interact with one another constantly, and they have a strong tendency to organize informal groups or an informality of formal groups. Among alumni, students of the same graduating class at high school develop the closest friendships. As a result, the Trust-Base Scale of these classmates is very high and is counted at the level of quasi-family members.

Classmates at the Military Academy are good examples. General Park Chung Hee was able to succeed in his coup d'état in 1961 mainly because he was supported by Colonel Kim Jong Pil, husband of General Park's niece, and Col. Kim's classmates of the Military Academy. These coup participants had a profound impact on the Korean politics, economy, and management. General Park became President and remained in that capacity until he was assassinated in 1979. Colonel Kim became one of the most powerful politicians in South Korea, and he still functions as a political power.

In 1980, General Chun Doo Hwan was able to grasp dictatorial power after a quasi-coup d'état simply because some of his classmates at the Military Academy supported him, and they participated in the fighting. General Chun became president, and his supportive classmates monopolized all the powers in South Korea for the next seven years. One of them, General Rho Tae Woo, became president after President Chun retired. Other participating classmates still remain as powerful dignitaries in South Korea.

As late as 1992, two cases of private organization of classmates of the Military Academy were uncovered. These organizations cause great apprehension among Koreans because they may attempt coup d'état whenever the Korean society becomes unstable. So as you can see, the case of the Military Academy signifies the importance of classmates in Korean society.

People from the same region demonstrate a strong solidarity in South Korea. Traditionally, Koreans have developed strong regional ties for many years because it is much easier to develop a close relationship with people from the same region. In both business and nonbusiness organizations, including the government, people from the same region maintain friendly relationships and help one another by organizing informal groups or an informality of formal groups. It is well known that the major political parties in South Korea are organized along regional lines. As a result, the Trust-Base Scale of regionalism is very high (70).

The Koreans are very cool toward strangers, both Koreans and foreigners (Bae 1992). Traditionally, the Koreans have developed a tendency to alienate themselves from unfamiliar things and strangers. This tendency might have originated because the Koreans have been one of the most homogeneous people in the world without affinity for strangeness. There are only 20,000 Chinese living in South Korea, the only alien residents in the country. Wysocki reported that one Korean Buddhist monk refused an interview with him by saying, "I don't want to look at a foreigner" (1987, p. 1). Even though this example might be extreme, it is undeniable that the Korean people are not comfortable with strangeness. As a result, the Trust-Base Scale of strangers and foreigners is one of the lowest (5 or 1). It is interesting to see that the Japanese share this view with Koreans. Lehner and Kanabayashi reported, "Some foreign businessmen say that they encounter Japanese purchasing managers who simply assume that no foreign product can even be as good as a Japanese product, and refuse even to look at samples" (1992, p. A12).

The Korean people fanatically abide by their established norms, which are determined socioculturally. The Koreans literally observe and respect these norms, and they cannot tolerate those who deviate from them. The Koreans are people of principle with little tolerance for flexibility and compromise. Korean Christians, for example, accept fellow church members wholeheartedly, but their Trust-Base Scale or acceptance level decreases significantly even with Christians from other churches of the same denomination. The Trust-Base Scale toward fellow Christians in different denominations is much lower than that of the same

Table 5.2
The Group Index

Subjects	Trust-Base Scale	Weight for Grouping	Group Index
Spouse	100	1	100
Parents	100	1	100
Children	100	1	100
Brothers/sisters	100	1	100
Nephews/nieces	99	1	99
Cousins	97	1	97
Relatives	96	1	96
Classmates of high school	97	10	970
Classmates of college	85	9	765
Classmates of elementary School	50	3	150
Alumni of high school and college	80	9	720
People with the same family name	70	9	630
People from the same region	70	8	560
People from different regions	60	4	240
People in the same job organization	90	9	810
People of the same profession	80	10	800
People with the same hobbies	70	7	490
Neighbors	70	5	350
Same church members	95	7	665
People in the same denomination	80	6	480
People in different denominations	70	5	350
People of different religions	40	4	160
Strangers (Koreans)	5	1	5
Foreigners	1	1	1

denomination simply because they believe that other Christians do not share exactly the same values which the Koreans cherish. Therefore, the Trust-Base Scale with people of different religions is very low.

Informal groups and informality of formal groups are organized in accordance with the Trust-Base Scale. However, we cannot completely organize groups until we add a weight for grouping. This concept implies the extent of initial intention to organize groups, the weight ranging from 1 to 10. While a score of 1 implies a weak tendency for group organization, a score of 10 implies a strong tendency for it. People with different backgrounds develop different tendencies toward grouping activities. A group index is then the product of a Trust-Base Scale and a weight for grouping, as shown in Table 5.2.

The weight for grouping by family members is very low in South Korea simply because they are ascribed group members (Daniels and Radebaugh 1989), although the family system is critically important and family members play an important role in chaebol enterprises and other businesses. In the initial stage of organizing a group, family members are not included. However, people with the same family name traditionally have a strong tendency to form groups.

Classmates and alumni have a very strong tendency to organize groups. The weight is very high specifically for groups of high school classmates. Traditionally, people from the same region or "doh" also have a strong tendency to organize groups. People from the same occupation have a high weight for grouping in informal groups. Strangers and foreigners have the lowest weight for grouping as a result of general human nature and the unique geopolitical and sociocultural environments of Korea.

The group index ranges from 1 to 1,000 (Trust-Base Scale of 100 × weight for grouping of 10). The highest group index is that of high school classmates (970), followed by people in the same occupational organization (810). The college classmates category is also important in forming groups. The group indexes of various family members are low because of the low weight of grouping. The scale of strangers and foreigners is one of the lowest because of the lowest Trust-Base Scale and weight for grouping.

CONCLUSIONS

The Korean people have developed a unique behavioral pattern which is different from patterns of other nations. It is imperative to understand the Korean behavioral pattern that relates directly to the management system in both business and nonbusiness organizations. We have proposed a conceptual framework of the Salad Bowl Group, the Trust-Base Scale, the I-We Consciousness Grid, and the Informality of Formal Groups as an attempt to establish a conceptual framework for the behavioral pattern of the Korean people.

We believe that we have proved that the Koreans have developed a behavioral pattern of individualistic and group activity simultaneously through the I-We Consciousness Grid and the Salad Bowl Group. We also believe that we proved that the Koreans have a tendency to pursue their individualistic interests through informal groups or informality of formal groups. The Salad Bowl Group, the Trust-Base Scale, the I-We Consciousness Grid, and the Informality of Formal Groups are useful tools for understanding this behavioral pattern. We again demonstrated the behavioral pattern of the Koreans to form friendships based on the Trust-Base Scale. Finally, we strongly encourage researchers to discuss this conceptual framework through statistical analysis from their own research.

Some Koreans insist that the individualistic behavior in a group setting is not a desirable behavior and has to be redirected toward one which is more group-oriented (Yun 1990). We have a different viewpoint concerning this matter. In the first place, it is not an easy task to change the traditionally held behavior of the majority of any people. We also have some reservations about those Koreans who claimed that the individualistic behavior is an undesirable phenomenon. To us, this individualistic behavior of the Koreans can go in either direction. It may have a negative connotation in that the Koreans may not be interested in the well-being of the entire society. However, this behavior has also many positive features. It will intensify severe competition among members of a group to attain personal goals. On the other hand, you must understand the concept of compromise in a group which has to be used strategically to achieve one's goals in a group setting.

The Korean management system is unique in the sense that the behavioral pattern of the Korean people is different from that of others and is a function of a behavioral pattern of its people, which has been formed socioculturally and geopolitically. The unique features of the Korean management system has been practiced by *chaebol* group corporations irrevocably in their management. In the next chapter, these chaebol corporations will be discussed extensively in order to disclose the unique features of the Korean management system.

REFERENCES

A President Committed Suicide because He Was Unable to Pay Workers' Wages. *The Dong-A Daily News* (September 3, 1992).

Bae, I. Korea's Antagonism to Outsiders is Too Excessive. *The Dong-A Daily News* (November 24, 1992).

Bruma, I. The Quarrelsome Koreans. *The New York Times Magazine* (March 26, 1988).

Cha, S. P. *Hankukui Kyungyung Nosakwankeh* (Labor–Management Relations in South Korea). Seoul: The Korean Chamber of Commerce, 1988.

Chang, C. S. Comparative Analysis of Management Systems: Korea, Japan, and the United States. In D. K. Kim and L. Kim (eds.), *Management behind Industrialization: Readings in Korean Business*, p. 241. Seoul: Korean University Press, 1989.

———. Chaebol: The South Korean Conglomerates. *Business Horizons* 31(2) (March-April 1988).

Daniels, J. D. and Radebaugh, L. H. *International Business.* Reading, Mass.: Addison-Wesley Publishing Company, Inc., 1989.

Darlin, D. Korean Labor Movement's Woes Raise Doubts about Its Survival. *The Wall Street Journal* (September 9, 1987).

Hasegawa, Y. Challenging Koreans. In I. G. Kim, *Hankuk, Munhwawa Kyungje Hwalryuk* (Korea: Its Culture and Economic Dynamism), p. 280. Seoul: The Korea Economic Daily, 1987.

Hayashi, S. *Kyngyunggwa Munhwa* (Management and Culture). (I. G. Kim, trans.). Seoul: The Korea Economic Daily, 1985.

Kim, D. K. and Kim, C. W. Korean Value Systems and Managerial Practices. In

D. K. Kim and L. Kim (eds.), *Management behind Industrialization: Readings in Korean Business*, p. 241. Seoul: Korea University Press, 1989.

Kim, I. G. *Yukyomunhwakuonui Jilseowa Kyungje* (The Social Order and Economy of the Confucian Culture). Seoul: The Korea Economic Daily, 1988.

Kim, T. K. *Hankukinui Gachigan Yungu* (A study of the Value System of Koreans). Seoul: Munumsa, 1982.

Kumon, J. Referred in T. Kusayanagi. Naui Hankukinkwan (My Perceptions of the Koreans). *The Dong-A Daily News* (October 18, 1980).

Kusayanagi, T. *Naui Hankukinkwan* (My Perceptions of Koreans). *The Dong-A Daily News* (October 18, 1980).

Lee, T. K. *Hankukinui Uisikkujo* (The Consciousness Structure of the Koreans). Vol. 1. Seoul: Munrisa, 1977.

Lehner, U. C. and Kanabayashi, M. Politician's Anti-U.S. Remarks Greeted with Silent Approval by Many Japanese. *The Wall Street Journal* (January 23, 1992).

Money Pools: It's There when Koreans Need It. *The New York Times* (September 29, 1986).

Murayama, M. Kazokushugi and Shudanshugi: Management Approach. *Sophia Economic Review* 19 (2, 3): 1973.

Safire, W. O-day Minus 300 in Korea. *The Index-Journal* (December 12, 1987).

Watanabe, T. *Hankuk Venture Jabonjuui* (Venture Capitalism in South Korea). (S. T. Kim, trans.). Seoul: The Korea Economic Daily, 1987.

Wysocki, B., Jr. South Korean Turmoil Has a Strong Element of Anti-Americanism. *The Wall Street Journal* (July 15, 1987).

Yun, C. K. Diagnosis of the Koreans. Series (19): The Koreans Lack Group Consciousness. *The Dong-A Daily News* (June 16, 1990).

6

Chaebol

James C. Abegglen (1973), an expert on the Japanese management system, was impressed that the Japanese economy grew twentyfold during the twenty-year period from 1950 to 1970. In 1950, the GNP per capita was barely $100, but it increased twentyfold to $2,000 in 1970. This is a phenomenal accomplishment by any standard.

South Korea accomplished the identical economic growth during the twenty-year period from 1965, when the GNP per output was just $100 to 1985, when it became $2,000 (Economic Planning Board 1985). South Korea's economy also grew 20 times in 20 years, although this occurred 15 years after Japan's. In both 1990 and 1991, the economic growth of South Korea was again impressive—the GNP growth rates were 9.3 percent and 8.4 percent, respectively, and the GNP per capita was $6,498 in 1991 (Bank of Korea 1992).

What is the driving force behind this phenomenal economic growth in South Korea? It seems that the following factors contribute to such an accomplishment:

1. Confucian ethics have been strictly implemented. This ethic is compatible with the Protestant work ethic in Western countries. Some elements of this work ethic are:

   - Hard work,
   - Respect for personal success,
   - Emphasis on education,
   - Enhancing family prestige and pride, and
   - Maintaining a stable and orderly society;

2. Government policy for economic growth and expansion has been generally successful since the early 1960s;

3. Determination of the Korean people (as workers and managers) to free themselves from absolute poverty;

4. Aggressive and talented entrepreneurs pursuing expansion for their businesses; and

5. Timely and skillful adaptation by government and business to the ever-changing international environment.

One of the key players in the phenomenal economic growth in South Korea has been entrepreneurs-businessmen. They are the dynamic resource converters by reacting and being proactive to dynamic and volatile domestic and international environments. Some of them failed in adapting to the environment and faded into obscurity. There are, however, entrepreneurs-businessmen who have survived and prospered. Some of them are quite successful and have established giant enterprises. In South Korea, they are called *chaebol,* which can be translated into "the conglomerate." You can see the importance of chaebol by knowing that they account for nearly 62 percent of the GNP of South Korea (Kraar 1992).

This chapter studies the characteristics of chaebol and their management system. The hypotheses of this study is that the management system of chaebol is based on FARS, where "F" stands for family relationships in their business, "A" for alumni relationships, "R" for regional relationships, and "S" for the state or government. The application of FARS concept is not unique in chaebol management, but the chaebol groups have used it effectively to their advantage to become giant enterprises.

DEFINITION AND POSITION OF CHAEBOL

According to the Fair Trade Commission (FTC) (1992), any enterprise can be considered as a chaebol when the total assets of the enterprise amount to 400 billion won ($533 million when the exchange rate is $1 to 750 won). The chaebol is comparable to the zaibatsu of Japan, and both chaebol and zaibatsu are spelled out by the same two Chinese characters.

Chaebol groups, as they are called in South Korea, are giant conglomerates by the South Korean standard. Some of the founding families of the groups are listed as billionaires by *Fortune* magazine (Sellers 1991 and Losee 1992). According to the FTC in 1992, there were 78 chaebol groups that ran 1,056 South Korean corporations.

Traditionally, chaebol groups are classified into the 50 largest, 30 largest, 10 largest, and 7 largest chaebol groups. According to the Report of the Ministry of Finance to the National Assembly (1992), chaebol groups based on the amount of their sales and the number of corporations they own or control in 1991 are shown in Table 6.1. In 1992, the

Table 6.1
Sales of Largest Chaebol Groups and Companies They Own

Rank in Sales	Chaebol groups	Sales ($ billion) ($1 to 780 won)	Companies
1	Hyundai	30.001	38
2	Samsung	27.139	49
3	Lucky-Goldstar	15.633	53
4	Daewoo	12.741	19
5	Sunkyong	8.734	29
6	Ssangyong	7.289	20
7	Kia	5.313	8
8	Hanjin	4.921	17
9	Hankuk Hwayak	2.919	21
10	Hyosung	2.792	14
11	Daerim	2.504	12

Source: Report of the Ministry of Finance to the National Assembly, October 13, 1992.

FTC designated 18 groups as new chaebol groups. One chaebol group dropped out because of the decrease in its total assets (Fair Trade Commission 1992).

THE MANAGEMENT PRACTICE OF CHAEBOL

The management system of any nation is a function of its own culture, and South Korea is no exception. The Korean culture is a subculture of the Chinese culture in which the Confucian values are strictly observed. Of course, the Korean culture has its own unique features that differ from those of both China and Japan, but the Korean management system, therefore, still shares features with them. However, it is different from the management systems of both of these countries in many ways.

In the Korean management system, relationships of family, alumni, region, and the state (government) are critically important. These relationships must also be important in the management systems of China and Japan. They are even somewhat important in the Western management systems, including that of the United States. However, they are uniquely crucial in the Korean management system. Without comprehending these relationships, no one can truly understand it. Chaebol groups and other business and nonbusiness organizations (military, government, schools, hospitals, etc.) have been using these relationships for their survival and expansion. In the following section, we discuss the impact of these relations on the Korean management system in general and the management of chaebol groups in particular.

FAMILY RELATIONSHIP IN CHAEBOL

The family relationship is crucial in the Korean management system because family prestige and pride is extremely important in the Korean society. No one has the liberty to bring disgrace upon his or her family prestige and pride. As part of the Korean management system, family relationship is a critical factor to chaebol. In almost all the chaebol corporations, the family members of the founders play key roles in the management of chaebol groups. In most cases, children of the founders hold the key positions in their organizations and one of them, usually the eldest son, succeeds his father once he retires or dies. Sons-in-law, fathers-in-law, uncles, brothers, and nephews also participate in the management of chaebol groups. There are, however, some chaebol groups in which relationship is not a crucial factor, but these groups are an exception to the rule.

The founder of Hyundai Group is Chung Ju Yung. He has seven sons who are called "seven princes." Among them, five sons now manage ten of the Hyundai corporations as top executives or are in top executive-track positions. One of the brothers of the founder, Chung Se Yung, is the chairperson of Hyundai Group after the founder retired from active management. Then he became the honorary chairperson of the group when he became a politician by organizing a political party. Now he has become a candidate for the presidency of South Korea. However, it has been speculated that Chung Mong Jun, the founder's sixth son, will eventually succeed his father. It is interesting to note that all four brothers of Chung Ju Yung, the founder, are now chairpersons of independent enterprise groups which became independent with assistance from their eldest brother after working with him for many years. Although they became independent, they mutually depend on one another for business transactions.

The founder of Samsung Group is Lee Byung Chull. Although this chaebol group has produced many professional career managers by applying Lee's philosophy of developing professional managers, his family members hold most of the important positions of the enterprise. Lee Kun Hee, the third son, took his father's position as chairperson after the founder's death. The second son and two sons-in-law hold the top management positions of Samsung Group. Two daughters of the founder became separated from the group after the oldest daughter took over Chunju Paper, and after the fifth daughter took over Shinsegye Department Store. Some speculated that this independence was a reaction to the government policy whose aim is to prevent the economic concentration by chaebol groups in South Korea.

Lucky–Goldstar Group is now a third-generation enterprise. Koo In Hwoi, the founder, died and his eldest son, Koo Cha Kyung, is now the chairperson of the group. His son, Koo Bon Moo, of the third generation, now a top executive member, is in line to succeed his father. Two uncles of the chairperson, the brothers of the founder, and two of his own brothers are key inner circle members of the group.

Miwon Group is one of the extreme cases in which many of the family members participate in the management of the enterprise. Even in South Korea where many family members are key players in the enterprise, Miwon Group is called a "family firm." The founder claimed that only family members can be trusted to be loyal to the organization, although they might be less capable than nonfamily members (Choi 1982).

As an exception among chaebol groups, the family members of Daewoo Group have never participated in the management of the enterprises, except for the wife of the founder. There are no grown children to participate in their father's business, and the founder refrains from indulging in a tradition of family participation.

Many of the second generations of the founding fathers of these enterprises have managed their group enterprises effectively by expanding their businesses. As an example, Kim Seung Youn, the chairperson of Hankuk Hwayak Group, succeeded his father when he was only 29 years old in 1981. At that time, there were 11 group corporations with total sales of 1,100 billion won, and with a net profit of 6.003 billion won. In 1989, eight years later, the number of group corporations was increased to 25, with sales of 3,150 billion won and with a net profit of 62.700 billion won. This impressive expansion was attributed to his influential leadership and effective management style (The Second Generation 1990).

Some of the third generation of chaebol groups are actively involved in the management of their family enterprises. The third generation of Lucky–Goldstar Group is a good example. All four sons of Koo Cha Kyung, the eldest son of the founder of the group and the chairperson of the group, are actively engaged in the management of their family enterprises. Koo Bon Moo, the eldest son of the chairperson, serves as the vice chairperson of the group, Koo Bon Nung, the second son, is vice president of a group corporation, Koo Bon Joon, the third son, is director of a group corporation, and Koo Bon Shik, the fourth son, is department manager of a company related to the group. Figure 6.1 shows the family lineage of Koo In Hwoi, the founder of Lucky–Goldstar Group.

Chaebol group families exert their efforts to strengthen their power and privilege by extending this tradition of family relationship in the Korean society into marriage. According to the survey of Seoul Kyungje Shinmun (1991), most of these chaebol group families have in-law relationships with the upper-upper class families in South Korea—families of influential politicians, high government officials, notable scholars, and financiers.

Figure 6.1
Family Lineage of Koo In Hwo

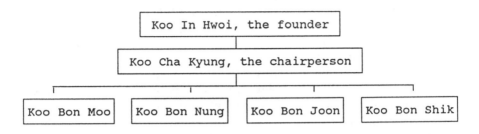

SCHOOL ALUMNI RELATIONSHIP IN CHAEBOL

Schools are important in any society, but in South Korea, they are crucial. As a whole, a Korean's career success depends on the schools from which he or she graduated. There are a number of very prestigious high schools and universities. In the past, a Korean had to graduate from Kyunggi High School and Seoul National University to guarantee career success. South Koreans call this guarantee "the K-S mark." Most leaders in government, business, and finance are those with the K-S mark. While there are other prestigious high schools and universities, a Korean must graduate from at least one of these institutions to achieve a successful career.

Chaebol corporations recruit management trainees mostly from the graduates of these prestigious universities. Daewoo Group is a good example. There are nine inner circle top executives who are vice chairpersons and presidents of the Daewoo corporations. Eight of them, including the founder of the group, are the alumni of Kyunggi High School.

Table 6.2 shows the universities that the inner circle top executives of the seven chaebol groups attended, excluding the founders and their successors.

Among the top executives of the seven largest chaebol groups, the alumni of Seoul National University account for 62.3 percent, and the three most prestigious universities (Seoul National University, Yonsei University, and Korea University) account for 84 percent of the top executives. This trend also applies to the middle and lower management levels of chaebol corporations, although the number of the graduates from other universities has increased among the top executives.

Many chaebol group corporations try to recruit graduates from prestigious universities. One method is to inform graduates of these universities of their employment in advance before the official employment

Table 6.2
Universities from which the Top Chaebol Group Executives Graduated

	Universities				
Chaebol	Seoul National U.	Yonsei Univ.	Korea Univ.	Military Academy	Others
Hyundai	1	3	3	–	–
Samsung	5	1	–	1	2
Lucky-Goldstar	11	1	–	–	3
Daewoo	7	1	1	–	–
Ssangyong	7	1	3	2	1
Hankuk Hwayak	6	–	–	–	1
Sunkyong	6	1	–	–	1
Total	43	8	7	3	8

Source: Bae In Joon, "The New Division Commanders of the Seven Chaebol Groups." The Shin Dong-A (April, 1985), pp. 524–548. Ro Hwan In, ed., Directory of Businessmen in Korea (1985). Seoul: The Federation of Korean Industries, 1985.

test day. However, these graduates are advised to take the test formally along with other job applicants. This practice may be irregular or unethical, but it is a desperate effort by the corporations to attract the most capable applicants.

Samsung Group, for example, employs 3,050 annually selected by the open employment test process. However, the group sends employment notification in advance to 80 graduates of Seoul National University and to about 40 graduates of Yonsei University. They are guaranteed employment, but they must also take the official employment test on the test day along with the other applicants. Hyundai Group attracts very capable graduates from prestigious universities by a similar method. The group guarantees employment to more than 300 graduates from prestigious universities. Since the competition for employment at large corporations is very keen, a guarantee of employment is the best news for job applicants. The number of job applicants usually outnumbers the positions offered by 7 or 8 times to 1 (Samsung Not Allowed 1990).

REGIONAL RELATIONSHIP IN CHAEBOL

Historically, the regional relationship is extremely strong in Korean society, and this tradition also applies to the management system. Al-

Table 6.3
Regional Origins of Chaebol Founders

Regions	Provinces, or doh	Numbers	Totals
Capital area	Seoul	7	
	Kyunggi	8	15
Central area	Chungbuk	3	
	Chungnam	7	10
Southwest area	Chunbuk	6	
	Chunnam	3	9
Southeast area	Kyungbuk	11	
	Kyungnam	13	
	Pusan	5	29
Northern area*	From 5 doh in North Korea		29

Source: Park Byung Woo, Chaebol and Politics (in Korean). Seoul: Doseo Chulpan Hankuk
  Yangseo, 1982, pp. 162–165.
*Businessmen whose original regions are in the Northern area of Korea (now North Korea)
  and who resettled in South Korea.

though the importance of the regional relationship has been somewhat weakened vis-à-vis family and alumni relationships, it is still significantly relevant to us for understanding the management of chaebol group corporations. In many cases, top level executives of chaebol groups are from the same region as the founders. The regional origins of the chaebol founders are shown in Table 6.3.

Before World War II, businessmen from the Southwest region dominated the Korean economy. After Korea was divided in half at the end of the war, businessmen from the Northern area (now North Korea) fled Communism and resettled in South Korea. They established the businesses that they abandoned in their original regions and expanded them into prosperous ventures. Dongyang Group is a typical example. Lee Yang Koo, the founder of the group, fled South from Communist North Korea and started a cement business. The sales revenue of the group was 600 billion won ($800 million at the exchange rate of $1 to 750 won) at the end of 1989 and they planned to sell 10 trillion won in ten years (The Second Generation 1990).

After the outbreak of the Korean Conflict, the businessmen of the

Table 6.4
Government Officials from Two Regions

	The Rhee Government	The Park Government	The Chun Government
Kyungsang doh (Southeastern)	18.8	30.1	43.6
Chunla doh (Southwestern)	6.2	13.2	9.6

Source: Hyundai Sahoi (Modern Society) Research Center.
Note: The Rhee government led by President Syngman Rhee; the Park government led by President Park Jung Hee; and the Chun government led by President Chun Doo Hwan.

Southeastern region prospered rapidly, simply because this region was the only area not invaded by the Communists from the North. The businessmen from this region found themselves blessed with this geographical advantage, which permitted them to develop their businesses into chaebol groups. Of course, they were very capable entrepreneurs. It is also important to mention that most political and military leaders since the early 1960s are also from this region, and it is easy to develop a close tie between the political leaders and the chaebol members from the same region. As a result, there are a great many chaebol groups from this region.

Koreans from other regions have discriminated against Koreans from the Southwestern region. Table 6.4 shows the disproportionate distribution of higher government officials in South Korea. The two former presidents and current president of South Korea are from the Kyungsang doh region, and they appointed many of the government officials from that same region as theirs at the expense of Chunla doh (the Southwestern region) in particular. Since both Kim Dae Jung and Kim Young Sam became candidates in the presidential election of December 18, 1992, the election again was a regional confrontation because Kim Dae Jung is from Chunla doh (the Southwestern region) and Kim Young Sam is from Kyungsang doh (the Southeastern region). Since Chung Ju Yung, the founder of Hyundai Group and the chairman of the United People's Party, was the third presidential candidate, regional confrontation among candidates was alleviated to some extent.

When chaebol groups recruit college graduates, they do not emphasize the regional relationship as strongly as they emphasize capacity and talent. However, college graduates will notice a subtle regional relationship as they climb up the organizational ladder of chaebol corporations.

STATE/GOVERNMENT RELATIONSHIP IN CHAEBOL

In the environment of South Korea, no businessman can become a chaebol group member without the support of government and political leaders. In a real sense, the chaebol groups are the products of a government-industry mix. Even though South Korea is a capitalist country, she has been under a government-led economy. This implies that the government and political leaders can create or destroy a chaebol group almost overnight. Samsung Group is a good example. Samsung Heavy Industries applied for producing commercial motor vehicles to the government. After much heated discussion within the government, the Department of Commerce and Industry finally decided not to allow the group to participate in producing commercial vehicles (Samsung Not Allowed 1992). As a result, the group missed an opportunity in the motor vehicle industry. The decision might prove to be a good one because three major car makers already exist in South Korea. However, the real issue is that business decisions of chaebol groups are not workable unless the government approves them. Businessmen, therefore, must maintain a close tie and a good relationship with the government and influential political leaders for their own success. However, the decision of the government vis-à-vis Samsung's commercial vehicles was reversed in 1992, and the government has allowed Samsung Group to produce commercial vehicles despite strong opposition from existing car producers such as Hyundai, Daewoo, and Kia (Samsung Planning 1992). It has been speculated that the government has yielded to the strong lobby of Samsung Group. Once again, this proves the relationship between the government and chaebol groups.

An area critically important for chaebol groups is one that raises and manages sufficient capital for the organizations which need loans from banks to obtain huge amounts of capital. The South Korean banking system, consisting of government-operated banks and commercial banks, is under tight control of the government. The simple truth is that you cannot continue your business unless you have loans from banks, and you cannot have loans from banks unless you maintain a good relationship with the government; no loans can be obtained without government approval, making chaebol groups and other corporations somewhat at the mercy of the government for their financing.

Table 6.5 shows outstanding loans of chaebol groups from banks, public and commercial. Total outstanding loans of the 30 largest chaebol groups banks amounted to 21.353 trillion won ($28.471 billion when the exchange rate was $1 to 750 won). These huge loans imply a unique feature of the financial structure of the management system in South Korea: a very high debt-equity ratio.

Table 6.6 shows debt-to-equity ratios of the major chaebol groups. Most

Table 6.5
Outstanding Loans of Chaebol Groups from Banks

Chaebol	Outstanding Loans from Banks	
Samsung	2.632 trillion won	($3.509 billion)
Hanjin	2.514	($3.352)
Daewoo	1.979	($2.638)
Hyundai	1.864	($2.485)
Lucky-Goldstar	1.683	($2.204)
Sunkyong	1.167	($1.569)

Source: The Bank Audit Commission, May 1, 1991.
Note: $1 = 750 won

Table 6.6
Debt-to-Equity Ratios of Chaebol Groups

			(1991)
Chaebol	Equity (billion won)	Debt (billion won)	Debt/Equity Ratio
Samsung	3,123	10,106	323.6%
Daewoo	2,562	7,638	298.1%
Hyundai	2,623	11,630	443.4%
Hanjin	446	6,300	1,412.6%
Lucky-Goldstar	2,147	7,623	355.1%
Sunkyong	1,688	4,122	244.2%

Source: Report of the Ministry of Finance to the National Assembly, October 13, 1992.

of these huge debts are bank loans, and the government strictly controls the banking business, including commercial banks. No chaebol groups are able to arrange loans from banks without government consent, and they are keenly aware that they cannot continue their businesses without these loans. Chaebol groups therefore have to maintain a good relationship with the government.

When the government decided to chastise Hyundai Group about the discord between them, the government applied its powerful weapon: discontinuation of bank loans to the group, who immediately felt the dreadful result of the government's action. The government then loosened this severe measure because of the great impact Hyundai has on the nation's economy.

Table 6.7
Ex-Government Officials Recruited by Chaebol Groups

| Chaebol | Occupation Before Joining Chaebol | | | |
	Politicians	Government	Military	Financiers
Samsung	–	1	2	1
Hyundai	–	2	3	2
Lucky-Goldstar	2	4	2	2
Daewoo	–	5	6	12
Sunkyong	–	1	–	1
Ssangyong	–	4	2	1
Hankuk Hwayak	–	7	3	1
Total	2	24	18	20

Source: Bae In Joon, "Ex-Bureaucrats and Ex-Military Men in the Business World." *The Shin Dong-A* (August, 1986), p. 403.
Note: All of them have positions of executive vice president and above in chaebol corporations.

There are many strategies for chaebol groups to maintain a good relationship with the government, one being to recruit ex-officials of the government, military, and financial world.

Table 6.7 shows how many of them were recruited for top positions by chaebol groups. This table indicates that chaebol groups extensively recruit ex-officials to their higher positions in an effort to maintain a close tie with the government. Chaebol founders and managers in chaebol group corporations are required to interact constantly with government leaders and officials for their successful business. The Blue House (the residence of the president), the ruling party, the National Assembly, the Economic Planning Board, the Ministry of Finance, and the Ministry of Commerce and Industry are especially relevant to them. The majority of government bureaucrats who joined chaebol groups are from these government departments.

Another important way for chaebol groups to maintain a good relationship with the government is to contribute donations to political leaders and the highest government officials, including the Blue House. In this quid pro quo, a chaebol group is guaranteed government support in return for its contribution. In other words, the contribution is a quasi-tax for the chaebol's survival and growth.

Table 6.8 shows the amount of contribution by the major chaebol

Table 6.8
Contribution by Major Chaebol Groups

Chaebol groups	Amount of Contribution	
Hanjin	13.307 billion won	($17.743 million)
Lotte	12.250	($16.333)
Ssangyong	11.540	($14.872)
Hyundai	9.074	($12.099)
Samsung	7.917	($10.556)
Sunkyong	7.667	($10.223)
Daewoo	7.117	($ 9.489)
Lucky-Goldstar	5.966	($ 7.955)

Source: Korea Internal Revenue Service, 1989.
Note: The exchange rate of $1 to 750 won was applied.

groups in 1988, the first year of the Rho Tae Woo government. Of course, not all of this donation was a political contribution for a quid pro quo, but South Koreans believed that a great portion of this contribution went to political and government leaders. The political contribution of a chaebol, for example, accounted for 24 percent of the net income. Some corporations had to donate even though they experienced loss in their net income. Without this contribution, they simply could not survive.

Chung Ju Yung, the founder of Hyundai Group, confessed officially that his group often donated to the Blue House. Sometimes, he donated two billion won ($2.7 million, at the exchange rate of $1 to 750 won), three billion won ($4 million), and five billion won ($6.7 million). After donating ten billion won ($13.3 million), he stopped providing political contributions. In his autobiography, Lee Dong Chan, the chairman of a chaebol group, noted that he also provided political donations to maintain a good relationship with political and government leaders for his enterprise.

LONG-TERM IMPLICATION OF FARS FOR CHAEBOL

A management system is a function of its culture, and the management system will change as the culture changes. We have witnessed that every culture changes slowly at times and rapidly at other times. The central concept of FARS in chaebol management will change somewhat over time. However, the main framework of this system will continue regardless of changes in environment.

The Korean culture is a stockpile of more than 2,000 years of heritage. The culture will abandon some of its components and absorb some new

Table 6.9
Professional Managers in Chaebol Groups

Chaebol	Total	The founder and his family members	Professional Career managers	Others
Hyundai	57	7	42	8
Samsung	41	2	28	11
Lucky-Goldstar	44	7	26	11
Daewoo	52	2	25	25
Sunkyong	26	3	21	2
Ssangyong	21	2	11	8
Hankuk Hwayak	21	1	9	11
Total	262	24	162	76

Source: Bae In Joon, "Ex-Bureaucrats and Ex-Military Men in the Business World." *The Shin Dong-A* (August, 1986), p. 403.
Note: These are executive vice presidents and above in the seven largest chaebol groups (as of July 15, 1986).

elements, but the basic framework of the culture will remain. The Koreans remain Koreans with their unique culture no matter what happens to them.

Many founders of chaebol groups are still in tight control of their enterprises, and in some groups, the second and even third generation family members participate in the management of their enterprises. As the chaebol groups expand their businesses, family members alone cannot control their entire enterprises. As a result, they need the help and support of many (nonfamily related) professional managers, although the most crucial key positions will continue to be held by the family members of the founders. This phenomenon is happening in chaebol groups, as Table 6.9 indicates.

More than 60 percent of the top-level managers in chaebol groups are nonfamily related professional career managers while family members account for less than 10 percent. Lee Myung Bak is one of the typical nonfamily-related, professional career managers in chaebol groups. Lee became a chairperson of Hyundai Construction Corporation, an important company of Hyundai Group. He managed to climb the organizational ladder of the group from a position of a regular employee. He has been called "the alter ego of Chung Ju Yung": The former is a grand-scale, bold entrepreneur; Lee is a genius professional manager. However, we should not be misled by these statistics. The founders and their direct descendants firmly control their chaebol enterprises. There are no signs that they will lose complete control in the near future. Daewoo Group may be the only exception among the many chaebol families.

Alumni relationship will remain strong in the management of chaebol groups in the future. So far, it has been proven by and large that a businessman's effectiveness in management correlates with the schools that he attended. Graduates of prestigious universities demonstrate greater effectiveness in management in the organizations of chaebol groups. All the chaebol group corporations, therefore, recruit management trainees mainly from the elite schools. It is almost impossible for any high school graduate or graduate of a nonprestigious college to climb the organizational ladder of chaebol group corporations unless he—not she—demonstrates extraordinary talents or is closely related to the founders of chaebol group corporations.

Regional relationships will maintain their place in the chaebol group corporations. Koreans insist on a stereotyped perception that each province or doh has characteristics different from those other provinces. A Korean from a certain province, for example, is different from other Koreans from another province, or doh in terms of accents, behaviors, attitudes, and even personalities. Some parents, for example, are extremely reluctant to have their children marry girls or boys from certain provinces. The founders and their top executives of chaebol groups favor those managers from the same region as they are because they believe that they have common values. The chaebol group leaders also anticipate strong commitment and loyalty from their subordinates of the same province.

In South Korea, some influential leaders exert their utmost efforts to alleviate traditionally held regionalism by claiming that the practice is harmful for the unity of the Korean people. Everyone agrees with them at least in part, but people also understand that it is an awfully hard task to free themselves from this bias. It is yet to be seen how powerful chaebol group corporations react to this call.

As the South Korean economy grows and expands, it will increasingly be a one-day radius economy through improvements in both the communication and transportation industries. It is, however, doubtful whether this long-cherished stereotyped perception will be affected in a significant way by this change in the society.

However, there are some signs of change in the government and chaebol groups. The government tries to regulate more aggressively in order to prevent the chaebol groups from becoming uncontrollable giant organizations. The government demanded that chaebol groups identify three corporations of major business lines in their groups.

Table 6.10
Three Corporations with Major Business Lines

Chaebol	Major Corporations	Proportion of Major stockholders
Samsung	Samsung Electronics	30.7%
	Samsung Chemicals	83.0
	Samsung Heavy Industries*	98.3
Hanjin	Korean Air	28.4
	Hanjin Marine Transportation	91.2
	Hanil Development	24.1
Daewoo	Daewoo, Inc.	14.9
	Daewoo Shipbuilding*	83.9
	Daewoo Electronics	7.1
Hyundai	Hyundai Motors Company	29.9
	Hyundai Electronics*	100.0
	Hyundai Petrochemical*	100.0
Lucky-Goldstar	Kumsungsa, Inc.	15.3
	Lucky, Inc.	10.8
	Kumsung Electronics*	100.0
Sunkyong	Yukong	26.3
	Sunkyong Industries, Inc.	30.4
	S K C, Inc.*	84.1

Source: Report of the Bank Audit Commission to the General Assembly, May 6, 1991.
*Corporations not listed in the stock market

Table 6.10 shows the three companies and the proportion of the major stockholders of the major chaebol groups. Through this realignment process, the government intends to accomplish many objectives. First of all, the government discourages extensive duplications of product lines by chaebol groups because it believes that extensive duplication weakens the competitiveness of South Korean products. Second, the government aims to prevent chaebol from becoming disproportionate giant enterprises. Third, the government decided to use this process to regulate the powerful influence of chaebol groups in business and possibly in politics.

THE SHOWDOWN BETWEEN THE RHO GOVERNMENT
AND HYUNDAI GROUP

Close ties between chaebol groups and the government will remain strong. As mentioned before, chaebol groups are the very product of the government, which provides extraordinary support and encouragement to their ventures. The basic assumption of government policy in the 1960s and 1970s was that only giant corporations could drive the nation's economy fast enough for growth and expansion. The South Korean government has, therefore, used chaebol groups as a means to expand the Korean economy. So, the government needs chaebol groups; they, in turn, need the government's support in the unique environment of Korean society. South Korea is a unique country in that many of the giant chaebol corporations are still at the mercy of the government and political leaders for their prosperity and even survival.

However, there is an indication that this relationship between the government and chaebol groups may change in the 1990s. The basic logic behind this change is that chaebol groups are now too powerful to be administered, and their economic concentration in the economy is too extensive to be manipulated. The Koreans are living in a period different from the 1960s and 1970s where strong government support was necessary for the growth of the Korean economy. Eventually, it will not be good for the South Korean economy to support discriminately in favor of chaebol groups. The government, therefore, must implement the policy of diffusing the mighty power of chaebol groups.

Chaebol groups responded and reacted fiercely to this policy and some, in turn, tried to maintain their powers by participating directly in politics themselves. This was an unprecedented phenomenon in South Korea. Hyundai Group is a good example. Chung Ju Yung, the founder and the former honorary chairperson of the group, organized a political party, the United People's Party, and won 32 seats of the General Assembly (Congress). He then became a candidate for the presidential election of December 18, 1992.

Chung's party has become a strong political party, and if Chung Ju Yung becomes president of South Korea, it will be really a government-chaebol mix. No longer will business and government be separated, but they will be integrated into a single entity. Chung will exercise his power on economy-politics, not economy and politics.

Government reaction is very swift and decisive. The Internal Revenue Service conducted an extensive tax audit of Hyundai Group and levied an additional tax of 136.1 billion won ($181.5 million at the exchange rate of $1 to 750 won). While the group accepted this amount, it has appealed to the tax court. In addition, prosecutors recently arrested some of the Hyundai executives on charges of evading taxes and forging company documents. Chung complained about the government's action. "Behavior by the administration before and after the general election (for the National Assembly) have convinced me that it wants Hyundai to collapse to satisfy its political greed in the coming presidential election" (Hyundai Destined 1992).

Through this showdown between the government and Hyundai, it will be clear whether or not the government really is capable of diffusing the power of the mighty chaebol groups for the good of South Korea. Or, perhaps the chaebol groups will form formidable political powers by participating directly in politics themselves and through their representatives. Already some chaebol group leaders have expressed their interests in participating in politics directly by supporting their people for the General Assembly (Congress).

Slowly and steadily, the honeymoon relationship between the government and chaebol groups has been changing. However, it is not yet clear in which direction this relationship is heading. In the next few years, it will become clear, however, whether the government can manipulate giant chaebol groups, or whether the latter will have become a dreadful dinosaur that no one, even the government, can control. Instead, the government and the society as a whole may be at their mercy.

PERFORMANCE EVALUATION OF CHAEBOL GROUPS

Since the founders of most chaebol groups were entrepreneurs, they were willing to challenge risk-taking ventures in Korea (before World War II) and in South Korea (after World War II). Originally, they started their businesses on a very small scale because they were usually small businessmen. Over time, they demonstrated their entrepreneurial talents under an extremely volatile geopolitical environment of South Korea. They are the entrepreneurs who challenged this unstable environment and turned it to their advantage.

Korea has encountered many risky and unstable environments, such as World War II, the division of Korea, the Korean Conflict, the ambitious expansionary economic policy of the military-rooted governments, the normalization of ties between South Korea and Japan, the participation in the Vietnam War, the oil shock, the devaluation of the U.S. dollar, student riots, the collapse of communism, and the change of government. These environments provided opportunities for many Korean (South Korean) entrepreneurs. Chaebol group founders not only survived these environments, but also prospered and greatly expanded their enterprises. This does not necessarily mean that they have always been successful, but their successes outweighed their failures and hard times.

During this period, many other entrepreneurs started their enterprises, but failed or remained as mediocre businessmen. However, most chaebol group founders and their successors have survived, and their enterprises have expanded through the use of their entrepreneurial talents. First of all, they have developed clear-cut visions for their ventures and developed many correct business lines. They then implemented their visions through carefully prepared strategic planning.

Second, chaebol group founders demonstrated successful political manipulation for their enterprises which is extremely crucial in South Korea. They had to convince the government and political leaders that their ideas and plans for their ventures are conducive to the expansion of the nation's economy. Once they succeeded in convincing the government officials, they in turn received enormous support from the government for their ventures, specifically in financing new ones. Chaebol group founders and managers understand clearly that they must have support from the government for their successful ventures. Many of them have been successful in this endeavor.

Third, chaebol group founders pursue their businesses aggressively. They created new corporations, added new product lines, bought and merged with existing corporations, and challenged competition vigorously in the domestic and international markets. For their successful accomplishments, they carried out their businesses with cool calculation, visionary insights, analytical capacities, and bold decisions.

Next, the founders and their successors proved themselves as good managers. Of course, each management style is different; while some of them are autocratic like Chung Ju Yung of Hyundai Group and the late Lee Byung Chull, others are more group-oriented like Koo Cha Kyung of Lucky–Goldstar Group. Some lie in-between like Kim Woo Choong of Daewoo Group. Most of them are good managers: They made good decisions through their own insights or through the help of inner-circle managers.

Last, chaebol groups have been blessed with good luck. They recognized opportunities, grasped them firmly, and applied them for their advantage, which brought their enterprises tremendous fortunes. Chaebol groups, for example, were blessed in the mid-1980s with the so-called "age of the three lows"; low oil price, low dollar value, and low interest rates. A low U.S. dollar is advantageous because the South Korean currency was devalued since it is pegged to the U.S. dollar. As a result, exports to other countries, and to the United States in particular, were brisk.

The 1990s will become the decade of challenge for most chaebol groups. For example, Samsung Group has become the most formidable non-Japanese Asian company and emerges as the most advanced technological powerhouse in South Korea. Lee Kun Hee, the chairperson of the group, works hard to transform Samsung Group into a competitor of Sony Corp. of Japan and General Electric Co. of the United States through his management style of decentralizing decision-making processes. However, the group must overcome a strong hurdle to achieve this goal: the technology gap between Samsung Group and its international competitors. The more the group succeeds in mustering technological prowess, the less it can expect the United States and Japan to share critical technologies. Nevertheless, Samsung Electronics Co., a company of Samsung Group, is now the second largest supplier worldwide of dynamic random-access memory (DRAM) chips. Only Toshiba Corp. of Japan produces more (The Korean Semiconductor 1992).

Daewoo Group restructured its organization after the group experienced a disappointing performance during a few years (Nakarmi 1991). The group must transform into a more effectively managed organization. Kim Woo Choong, the chairperson, exercised a drastic measure by taking centralized control and streamlining management at his group. Kim retired scores of senior executives for their poor performances and easygoing manner. He also fired nearly 200 middle managers in a Daewoo Group subsidiary.

However, Daewoo Group has to establish a firm strategy for a strategic dilemma. The group has not yet achieved a dominant position in any single industry unlike other major chaebol groups and has also lagged in establishing its brand name.

The result of the showdown between Hyundai Group and the government after the presidential election in December, 1992 will redefine the position of chaebol groups in the Korean society. If the government fails to manipulate Hyundai Group, it signifies that chaebol groups in general have become too large to be controlled. Meanwhile, Hyundai Group is adjusting itself to grow and expand under this unpredictable environment. The group, for example, plans to move its personal computer business to the United States (Carlton 1992). Instead of simply distributing Korean-made products, Hyundai will design and assemble personal computers (PCs) in its San Jose, California, plant which will make it easier for them to respond to rapid changes in the American market (Eng 1992). Since Japan and the United States, the two most advanced countries in technology, are reluctant to transfer their technology to South Korea, the best strategy is to operate their plants in the United States by accessing the most advanced technology.

The rest of the chaebol groups are closely watching the result of the showdown between the government and Hyundai Group, which will have a major impact on them. Most chaebol group leaders agree in principle about the separation of business and politics and are reluctant to get involved directly in the latter. They clearly understand, however, that politics is a part of their lives for their enterprises. In one sense, they have been forced to get involved in the South Korean political process, either directly or indirectly.

CONCLUSIONS

Chaebol groups have firmly established themselves in South Korea in a very short time period and will have a tremendous impact on the nation's economy and society. They have contributed significantly to the growth and expansion of the economy, and most Korean people have benefited from them through the employment and the goods and services they provide. However, this growth has caused unequal distribution of wealth among Koreans. Many worry about the domination of chaebol groups in business and even in politics as well as about the socioeconomic polarization of the society. These concerns have sparked street demonstrations by unconvinced radical students and workers.

The management of chaebol groups through FARS has proved effective in their management. However, this management practice has brought some negative side effects. In many chaebol groups, cooperation among family members has been satisfactory, but there are some unfortunate cases. In Miwon Group, for example, there was a $10 million lawsuit between the founder and his younger brother (Miwon Founder Resigned 1986), as well as family feuds in other chaebol groups, which jeopardized their business operations.

Emphasis on the graduates of the prestigious universities has brought many capable managers to the chaebol groups. A friend of ours, who is one of the top executives of Lucky–Goldstar, confirmed this practice personally when we visited him for an interview in 1987. It is generally agreed that the practice works very well in Korean society. This emphasis also has produced dysfunctions. All the college-bound high school students aspire to attend one of the few prestigious Korean universities, but the capacities of these institutions are very limited. This produces many undesirable social problems to Korean society, such as widespread dissatisfaction with the establishment. Some of the chaebol groups have tried to minimize this problem by establishing a recruiting policy of hiring any capable applicant regardless of education or the university he or she attended. So far, this reform has received a cool reception by other chaebol groups.

Regional relationship brings about cohesiveness in chaebol corporations, and every South Korean understands that it is almost impossible to extinguish the characteristics that Koreans have attached to each province for so many years. Chaebol corporations simply admit this long tradition and apply it for their benefit. However, this has resulted in some uncomfortable relations among the Koreans in different provinces. Some chaebol corporations are reluctant to promote some managers simply because they are from a certain province or doh, regardless of their capacity. This is really a civil rights issue. Many business and nonbusiness leaders have expressed their concerns over this unfounded prejudice or practice, which is not expected to fade away in the foreseeable future.

The relationship between the government and chaebol groups has produced the so-called, "Miracle of Han River," making South Korea one of the frontrunners among the newly developed countries in economic growth. The government has given extensive support to chaebol groups in order to achieve government goals, and the chaebol groups did their part. With the help and encouragement of the government, they expanded their enterprises and created new business lines through careful yet bold planning and implementation.

There has been, however, much criticism about this government policy. Is it wise to create a few extremely wealthy people at the expense of the rest of the population, even though chaebol groups have contributed to economic growth and prosperity? Is it not more desirable to have development balanced between large and small businesses? This is a very serious social and economic issue in South Korea, and there seems to be no correct solution for it. This failure to find solution may lead to instability in the society.

Chaebol groups are at the crossroads. The Rho Tae Woo government began to weaken the mighty power of chaebol groups because the government leaders believe that these groups will not serve the good of the Korean people. They fear that chaebol groups will eventually dictate Korean society not only in business, but also in all the aspects of the Korean society. The response from chaebol groups is direct and official, but they maintain that business and politics should not be mingled too closely. However, the government leaders must respond to the question of controlling chaebol groups.

The effective use of both human and nonhuman resources can achieve effective management. If the Korean management system is different from any other management systems, its uniqueness usually comes from its human resource management which we will discuss in the next chapter.

REFERENCES

Abegglen, J. C. *Management and Worker, the Japanese Solution.* Tokyo: Sophia University, 1973.

The Bank of Korea. *The Preliminary Statistics of the Economy of 1991.* Seoul: The Bank of Korea, 1992.

Carlton, J. Hyundai Plans to Move its Division for Personal Computers to the U.S. *The Wall Street Journal* (April 20, 1992).

Choi, C. L. *The 24 Hours of Chaebol* (in Korean). Seoul: The Economic Department of the Chosun Daily News, 1982.

Economic Planning Board. *Major Statistics of Korean Economy, 1985*. Seoul: Bureau of Statistics of Economic Planning Board, 1985.

Eng, P. M. Made in the U.S.A. . . . by Hyundai. *Business Week* (October 26, 1992).

The Fair Trade Commission. *The Designated Large Enterprises in 1992*, 1992.

Hyundai Destined for Collapse, Says Chung. *Korea Times* (April 27, 1992).

The Korean Semiconductor Boom Boomerangs. *Business Week* (October 5, 1992).

Kraar, L. Korea's Tigers Keep Roaring. *Fortune* (May 4, 1992).

Losee, S. The Billionaires. *Fortune* (September 7, 1992).

Miwon Founder Lim, D. H. Resigned. *The Dong-A Daily News* (November 29, 1986).

Nakarmi, L. At Daewoo, a "Revolution" at the Top. *Business Week* (February 18, 1991).

Samsung Not Allowed to Participate in Commercial Vehicles. *The Dong-A Daily News* (August 22, 1990).

Samsung Planning Commercial Vehicles Venture. *The New York Times* (June 13, 1992).

The Second Generation of Chaebol Groups. *The Dong-A Daily News* (March 28, 1990).

Sellers, P. The Billionaires. *Fortune* (September 9, 1991).

Seoul Kyungje Shinmun. *Chaebolkwa Kabol* (Chaebol Groups and Marriage). Seoul: Jishik Sanupsa, 1991.

7

Human Resource Management

The economic growth of South Korea is very impressive despite political instability and furious labor strife in recent years. According to the Bank of Korea (1992), the growth rates in the GNP were 6.8 percent in 1989, 9.3 percent in 1990, and 8.4 percent in 1991.

What is the driving force behind this phenomenal economic growth in South Korea which accomplished this miracle with very little natural resources? We believe that the driving force is the determination of the Korean people to achieve strong economic growth. We also believe that they have the capability to accomplish this goal. By "the determination of the Korean people," we mean that there has been consensus among the Korean people; the government leaders and officials, entrepreneurs, managers, and employees are all determined to achieve economic growth and to free themselves from persistent hunger and poverty. The Koreans are capable of accomplishing impressively high economic growth because they are highly educated and talented people who place a high value on success.

Business corporations alone cannot accomplish economic growth. This growth results from a collective effort from the entire population in a society with an effective combination of capitalism and government policies. Therefore, this growth must be understood in the context of a synergistic approach. In order to achieve this goal, all of the leaders and managers in South Korea, including the government, schools, corporations, and nonbusiness organizations, should turn themselves into effective resource converters. By "resource converters," we mean the use of available resources, both human and nonhuman, in order to achieve their prospective goals so that the nation as a whole can achieve overall economic growth. The society has to transform itself into "South

Korea, Inc." at least until the foundation for economic growth is firmly established.

This chapter will study the practice of human resource management by both business and nonbusiness organizations in South Korea and will cover all of the areas of human resource management in the context of its environment. This study was conducted through secondary data from Korean language resources and extensive interviews with the top executives and personnel managers of two *chaebol* group corporations, the president and the personnel manager of a medium but well-managed company, and the director of nursing of a large university hospital in 1987 and 1991.

We believe that the Korean people and their culture must be comprehended for a better understanding of their human resource management. Some of the concepts were discussed in the previous chapters.

KOREAN PEOPLE AND THEIR CULTURE

The Korean human resource management may differ from the practices of other countries because the Koreans have their unique national characteristics and culture. The geopolitical environment and various indigenous religions have influenced and formed the characteristics of the Korean people and their culture. Many religions, such as Shamanism, Buddhism, Taoism, and Confucianism, all have influenced the characteristics of the Korean people in one way or another.

There are typical characteristics of the Korean people and their implications to human resource management. First, the Korean people have developed a conflict personality of individualism and group activities. While they are very individualistic, they are also dedicated members of many groups and organizations. The Koreans, therefore, exercise confrontation to pursue individualistic interests and compromise in order to act as members of groups and organizations. Constant exercising of confrontation and compromise dominates their lifestyle in their everyday life and balancing them does not come easy. Extensive labor strife and violent student demonstrations are also representational characteristics.

The Korean people have a tendency to express their individualistic aspirations by informal groups and the informality of formal groups. Some of the more noticeable bases for informal groups consist of the family, alumni, and their original regions. We referred to them as FAR (Family, Alumni, and Regionalism), and the FAR plays an important role in the management of human resources in organizations.

The Korean people sternly abide by their established norms, which are determined culturally and socially, and they must observe and respect them literally, while not tolerating those who deviate from them. The Koreans are people who show a minimal spirit of flexibility and compromise because they are principled and rigid. Human resource management in South Korea can be effective only when it complies with these norms of behavior.

The Korean people understand clearly their position in their society and in their families. They also respect those persons above them in the hierarchical order and treat their subordinates properly. They also endeavor to maintain a good relationship with their colleagues in lateral order by emphasizing trustfulness. This tendency contributes to a stabilizing factor in the Korean society regardless of the outward turmoil. In many cases, the Korean people sacrifice their personal interests to meet the requirements of the hierarchical or lateral orders in society and in their organizations. This stability factor and the principle of reciprocity are critically important in understanding human resource management in South Korea.

To most Koreans, enhancing family prestige and pride is a supreme obligation. Just as the Korean people exist in order to enhance their family prestige, it is an unforgivable sin for anyone to disgrace his or her family. In the Korean society, individuals are motivated to strive for personal career success in order to enhance family prestige and pride. The aspirations of chaebol group founders and candidates of presidential elections should be understood in this context, in addition to other considerations. This family prestige and pride is also relevant to human resource management because employees are motivated to have a career success to enhance their family prestige and pride.

Education is extremely important. Education makes it possible for one to achieve personal career success, which brings family prestige and pride. The Korean society strictly observes the formula: education equals success. In every sense, providing a good education for their children is a supreme obligation of parents, the education of their children being really a family business. Parents, and mothers in particular, sacrifice everything in order to provide a good education for their children. Under this environment, South Korea has produced many educated people. This reservoir of highly educated people presents one of the definite reasons for the impressive economic growth of South Korea. Education is important in human resource management in that highly educated people are more motivated and more effective in organizations.

The Korean society resembles an open society because no rigid class society exists. Anyone can succeed in a venture or career if he or she is a hard working, capable person. Some of the founders of chaebol groups came from very poor families having only a grade-school education, emphasizing that everyone has equal opportunities. However, discrimination against women prevails even today in Korean society, making it almost impossible for women to climb the organizational ladder to the top positions except for teachers and professors, or in female-dominated professions such as nursing. The FAR concept mentioned previously will have an adverse impact on this open society for equal opportunity. In human resource management, the open society is still relevant because it provides relatively equal opportunities to anyone who tries to succeed in organizations.

Under the influence of Buddhism, the Korean people have cherished mercy towards their fellow human beings. They have been indoctrinated not to kill arbitrarily even small insects. They entertain uninvited guests and beggars generously. Under the influence of Confucianism, they have been encouraged to behave like Oriental gentlemen by showing their benevolent behavior to other people. The Koreans call it "in" or "induck," meaning a virtuous life. However, no single religion dictates the life of the people as Islam does to the Arab people and as Judeo-Christianity to the Western World. Instead, the Korean people show great tolerance toward many other religions. This behavioral pattern is relevant to human resource management because Korean employees and managers can interact with fellow workers without any restrictions. This lack of restrictions contributes to increased productivity.

The Korean people are the most homogeneous people in the world. They comprise the same race, use only one language, and eat the same food. To them, there is no room for strangeness in their mentality, and it is difficult for them to understand diversified and pluralistic societies like the United States. In human resource management, managers and workers take this homogeneity for granted, and it is difficult for foreigners employed as managers in organizations in South Korea. South Korea is the only country in Asia where there are only a handful of Chinese residents, and their number has been declining steadily.

Now that we have reviewed the Korean people, their culture, and its relevance to human resource management, we will discuss the unique features of human resource management, the characteristics of the Korean people, and their culture providing a basis for it.

THE UNIQUE FEATURES OF HUMAN RESOURCE MANAGEMENT IN SOUTH KOREA

There exist many features in the practice of human resource management in South Korea. First of all, government intervention and manipulation prevails very strongly in human resource management in general, and in labor unions and wage administration in particular. The government justified these interventions and manipulations in the name of the national goal of growth first and distribution later. The Rho Tae Woo government, in which wage increases were in the double digits, dramatically reversed this policy. Average wage increases nationwide were 21.1 percent in 1989 and were an estimated 17 percent in 1990. The government announced guidelines calling for wage increases in 1991 to be below 10 percent in order to prevent rapid increases in wages (South Korea's Wage Guidelines 1990).

Most chaebol group corporations and other organizations prefer recruiting as management trainees the graduates of prestigious universities in the Seoul area. However, there are discriminatory practices in human resource management in South Korea. For example, corporations traditionally practice discrimination against female employees in that employers usually do not recruit women for upper-management positions. Furthermore, once a woman worker marries, she resigns from her job. Marriage means retirement from their jobs for many female employees even though the Constitution and labor laws guarantee equal employment opportunities. Managers in female-dominated professions, as well as teachers and professors in educational institutions, however, maintain their positions even after they marry. This discriminatory practice has been alleviated somewhat in recent years because of a severe labor shortage in South Korea and the government's emphasis on equal employment opportunities for women. Four companies, for example, were prosecuted by the government when they advertised to recruit male applicants only in the newspapers (Male Only 1990).

Corporations and nonbusiness organizations have begun to hire married women, and this signifies a new trend in human resource management in South Korea. Table 7.1 shows the percentage of employment by occupation and sex in 1983 and 1990. According to the Economic Planning Board (1990), 8.462 million women were employed in 1990, and 8.4 percent of them were in professional and managerial jobs. Discrimination also occurs because a wide range of wage and salary differences exists

Table 7.1
Employment by Occupation and Sex (Percentage)

Occupation	Male		Female		Total	
	1983	1990	1983	1990	1983	1990
Professional and Managerial	7.3	9.6	4.1	8.4	6.1	9.1
Clerical	11.4	14.1	9.2	13.9	10.5	14.0
Sales	13.4	13.7	18.7	18.8	15.5	15.6
Service	6.6	7.7	15.4	18.6	10.1	12.0
Agriculture and Fishery	27.5	14.1	32.5	12.5	29.4	13.5
Manufacturing and Transportation	33.8	40.8	20.1	27.8	28.9	35.8

Source: Economic Planning Board, 1990.
Note: Figures in 1990 were as of February.

between college graduates and their high school counterparts. On the average, the wage and salary of high school graduates is about 60 percent of their college counterparts (Salary Discrepancy 1987).

Another feature of Korean human resource management is that some disciplines such as engineering, law, business, and some languages such as English, Russian, Chinese, and Japanese have become highly marketable areas. Hence, graduates of other disciplines will experience difficulty in obtaining jobs. Yet another characteristic is the fact that family members of the founders of corporations and nonbusiness organizations hold key positions in organizations, even though some efforts have been made to correct such practices.

Most chaebol group corporations recruit new employees in June and November each year. Since the school year ends in December, November recruiting takes on a major scale. Other small and medium companies recruit new employees after chaebol corporations complete their recruitment. Employees work six days a week, Monday through Saturday, and until two o'clock in the afternoon on Saturdays. The system of working every other Saturday is spreading among corporations and nonbusiness organizations. The system of five working days a week is used in some organizations. Employees worked 46.3 hours per week in 1991, a significant reduction from 52.5 hours in 1986. According to the Korea Labor Research Center, 1991, these are the longest working hours in the world. Also, there is a delay of compensation payment of wages and salaries for several months which still prevails in some small and medium companies. Whenever necessary, corporations and nonbusiness organizations lay off their workers and managers, but employees also change their jobs freely. The turnover rate is, therefore, relatively high in the Korean management system.

One final feature of Korean human resource management is that Korean tradition and the influence from both Japan and the United States have influenced the practice of human resource management systems in South Korea. While Japan occupied Korea for 35 years officially until the end of World War II, the Japanese introduced modern management system and human resource management practices to Koreans. Since the War, the United States has influenced South Koreans in every aspect of life, including the management system and human resource management practices.

RECRUITING AND SELECTING

Recruiting

Based on the planning of human resource management, the recruiting and selecting processes take place twice a year for chaebol corporations. Non-chaebol group corporations usually recruit officially once a year

Table 7.2
Recruiting Practice by Chaebol Corporations

Corporations	Recruiting				Number of	Date of
	1992	1991	1990	1989	Applicants	Selection
Hyundai	2,500	n.a.	n.a.	2,500	15,000*	November
Samsung	2,650	2,650	3,050	2,930	20,000*	November
Lucky-Goldstar	1,200	1,650	1,800	1,600	11,000*	November
Daewoo	1,250	1,000	n.a.	2,150	15,000*	November
Sunkyong	370	450	450	450	n.a.	November
Ssangyong	400	500	550	600	n.a.	November
Hanjin	362	550	500	450	n.a.	November
Hankuk Hwayak	400	500	500	550	n.a.	November

Source: The Dong-A Daily News (October 6 and 19, 1987, October 27, 1989, September 5, 1991), and The Hankuk Daily News (October 5, 1992).
*Number of applicants as of 1987.

Table 7.3
Recruitment of Non-Chaebol Corporations

Schools	All recruits	Male	Female
College	20,098	19,090	1,008
Technical college	6,557	5,386	1,171
High School	137,919	63,000	74,919

Source: The Ministry of Labor, 1987.

after the November recruiting by chaebol group corporations. Table 7.2 presents the recruiting practices of some chaebol group corporations. The competition for employment by major chaebol corporations is extremely intense for college graduates. Approximately 154,000 college graduates applied for 60,000 job openings in 1986 (Colleges Worry about Jobs 1986). According to the survey of 6,516 non-chaebol group companies with more than 100 employees by the Ministry of Labor, 2,065 of them plan to employ 165,574 graduates of various schools as Table 7.3 illustrates.

Female graduates account for 46.8 percent of all recruits. However, women account for only 5 percent of the college graduates. This practice verifies that corporations are reluctant to recruit women as management trainees in their organizations.

Although intense competition exists for career employment for college graduates, a shortage of manpower in some critical areas of business and engineering plagues some corporations. According to the data of the Human Resource Bank of Korean Employers' Federation (A Survey of Job 1987), only 1,941 applied for 2,180 positions in these areas.

In 1987 when we interviewed the nursing director of a hospital with 500 beds, one of the largest hospitals in the nation, she explained that there was a glut in the reservoir of registered nurses. Her hospital recruited 40 nurses from 600 registered nurses who applied for the positions. In 1987, the Yonsei Medical Center advertised seven openings for staff positions and 111 applied for them. For the positions of 20 technicians, 488 applied (1987).

Recruiting organizations advertise through a combination of the following methods:

1. Newspaper advertisements of openings,
2. Placement centers at various schools,
3. Job positions advertised in factories for manufacturing workers, and
4. Personal references.

Applicants for the jobs submit the following documents to recruiting organizations:

1. An application form with an attached photo,
2. Resume,
3. School transcripts,
4. Professor or teacher recommendations,
5. Proof of completing army duty (for male applicants only), and
6. Other supporting documents such as a copy of professional licenses.

Selecting

The selection process of business and nonbusiness organizations is based on a combination of the following methods:

1. Document evaluation,
2. Written tests of English and major concentration area,
3. Dexterity tests if applicable,
4. Aptitude tests,
5. Recommendations,
6. Interview, and
7. Physical examination.

Shin (1988) confirmed the importance of the concept of the FAR (Chang 1988) in the recruiting and selecting processes. He stated that, in quite a few companies, over 80 percent of their employees are from a particular region. This fact shows sufficient evidence that a person's hometown region has a critical influence on the process of his or her employment. In terms of kinship, the actual portion of those hired out of the total number of employees may be small. However, those related to the owner or executives are easily hired.

Some of the major chaebol group corporations use the following selection processes for their applicants.

Samsung	Written tests, interview
Lucky–Goldstar	Written tests, interview
Daewoo	Internship
Sunkyong	School recommendation, written tests, interview
Ssangyong	Document evaluation, written tests, interview
Hanjin	Document evaluation, written tests, interview
Hankuk Hwayak	Document evaluation, written tests, interview

Since the system was introduced officially by Lucky–Goldstar Group in 1984, internship plays an important role for some major chaebol group corporations. In the selection process, these corporations treat preferentially those applicants who worked for them through an internship program. Daewoo Group, for example, officially hired 1,000 new employees out of 1,400 interns (Personality 1991). In 1992, major chaebol groups plan to hire approximately 5,000 new employees through this internship system, including the following chaebol groups.

Daewoo Group	Approx. 1,500
Samsung Group	Approx. 1,000
Lucky–Goldstar Group	Approx. 400
Pohang Iron and Steel	Approx. 400

This internship system has many advantages for both corporations and applicants. Through this internship, corporations are able to predict the capacity of prospective employees, and internship students are almost guaranteed employment in the corporations where they interned. Therefore, they do not have to prepare for the job examination. However, this internship deprives other college seniors who were not selected as internship students from having an equal employment opportunity. Most internship students are from the most prestigious universities in the Seoul area.

TRAINING AND DEVELOPMENT

After corporations select their needed manpower, training and development programs begin right away with orientation programs.

Orientation Program

Every organization in South Korea has orientation programs, and major chaebol group corporations have extensive ones. Hyundai Group, for example, has a four-week orientation program in Seoul and Ulsan, which covers 62 subjects in 184 hours. The curriculum includes moral education (36.8%), organizational life and physical fitness (26.2%), visiting work places (21.2%), and basic job knowledge (15.8%). Hyundai also sends newly hired employees to remote villages and requires each employee to sell the company products. Another popular orientation program is a simulation of the investment of 200 million won in small groups.

Samsung Group has a comprehensive training center in Yongin and a 24-week orientation program. Lucky–Goldstar Group has a two-week orientation program in Inchon and Lichon, followed by one week of computer education and three weeks of group education. In the last stage of orientation, new employees participate in physical training by walking 50 kilometers (31 miles) and climbing mountains. Daewoo Group has a 10-night, 11-day orientation program in Buchon and Inchon. Simulation of investing 100 million won by five or six members, lectures, and visiting various sites of the company form the main content of the program.

Training and Development

Training and development of their employees comprise the major interests of top executives since it is only in this way that they can increase productivity and maintain competitiveness. To this end, large chaebol group corporations have developed training and development programs for their employees. Hyundai Group established the Manpower Development Center in 1980 and reeducated 21,000 college-educated employees. The center tries to enhance international competitiveness through management training, short-course Industrial College, foreign language training, and an international business seminar. The group's policy makes it mandatory that college-educated employees take Special Comprehensive Education at the center once every three years. A one-month program consists of 180 hours, including 70 hours of English and 110 hours of job-related training. The result of the training in terms of the subsequent test scores corresponds directly to promotion and bonuses.

Bonuses of 50 to 450 percent of regular salary depend on test scores.

Samsung Group also emphasizes the importance of training and the development of human resources. The group established a one-year course at the Samsung Academy, which reeducates 50 managers at a time. The group also established a two-year college course that concentrates on management and trade for 100 mid-level managers.

The company college is gaining popularity among employees. Six of them exist to educate their employees. The well-established Hanjin Industrial College of Hanjin Group is a typical example, and its main objective is to educate employees who have only high school diplomas. Once they graduate from this college, they are treated as equals of the employees who have college degrees in terms of promotion and compensation. In 1990, this group spent 15 billion won ($20 million at the exchange rate of $1 to 750 won) on training and development.

This training and development extends to off-the-job training as well. A little more than 40 employees of Samsung Group, for example, were sent to the United States, Japan, and Europe to complete masters degree programs in the areas of semicomputers and bioengineering. Lucky–Goldstar Group selects promising employees and sends them to prestigious universities around the world to earn masters degrees within two years, and doctoral degrees within five years. Daewoo Group also sends their employees to overseas universities. Through this program, 114 employees earned a masters degree and 86 of them earned a doctoral degree. The group has established a blueprint of employing 1,000 doctoral degree holders.

Language training has been emphasized in training and developing employees. One company, for example, offered a one-year course in English and Japanese. Each evening after work, employees would spend about two hours in taking English or Japanese lessons. Hyundai Group has added a Russian language course for their business in the Russian Republics.

The Foreign Language University in Seoul is a popular place for off-the-job training of foreign languages. Many of the government's civil servants and employees of corporations take English, Japanese, Chinese, French, Spanish, Arabic, Malay, Russian, and Indonesian. A group of 100 of them spend five months together at the university for their language training. Another group of 90 students takes lessons for five months after work.

In order to maintain the competitive edge in the global market, some companies have developed unique strategies. One company, for example, sent several promising employees to foreign countries without any specific work assignment for one year because they believe that the best training is learning in a local environment. They stayed in foreign countries, mingling with local people and speaking local languages. Through this method, these employees learned local cultures, business patterns, customer behaviors, government-business relations, and languages.

The government also strongly endorses training and development in organizations by making it the government policy for corporations with more than 150 employees to establish a training center for them. Small companies, however, experience an extensive financial burden in operating the training center.

This training and development, however, also has negative side effects — stress and tension for employees. As in Hyundai Group, training and development correspond directly to promotion and compensation in South Korea in many occupations. Government officials, managers in financial and banking institutions, and large corporations must take an examination for promotion. If they fail to pass these examinations, their promotions are curtailed, demoralizing them. Some of them even changed jobs to escape the humiliation. Some employees even rent apartments near their work place to fulfill extensive training requirements of their organizations.

EVALUATION AND PROMOTION

Evaluation

Evaluation is an important function in human resource management because it corresponds directly to promotions and to salary increases. It is commonly practiced in South Korea but it differs from those of other countries because of the unique environment of organizations in South Korea. First of all, a seniority system prevails strongly in South Korea, which may restrict the literal application of an objective evaluation system. It is, therefore, an open question whether or not both employees and managers take the formal evaluation process very seriously. When we questioned the usefulness of the evaluation process, most of the personnel managers responded that it was just one of the basic sources of information in the evaluation process. Yet, they presented us with well-prepared evaluation forms, most of which shared questions about an employee's performance, capability, attitude, personality, and work habits and have approximately 15 items covered under the broad subjects mentioned above. Two or three superiors often evaluate each employee at a time.

Evaluation in South Korea is different in that the "yonkong" management system is based on seniority. Some scholars and managers (Yang and Park 1991) have criticized this practice and have urged a change from the yonkong system to a merit or performance evaluation system. They claim that the seniority system has failed to gauge the employee's capability as well as his performance and contribution to the organization.

Daewoo Group (Nakarmi 1991), however, fired 200 middle managers based on the traditional evaluation system because of their ineffectiveness in the organization. This signifies that the traditional evaluation system is still working in the Korean management system. We have experienced both the advantages and disadvantages of the evaluation system based on merit and performance, and our opinion is that it is not a panacea. A system representing compromise of the seniority system and the merit/performance evaluation system may be needed in human resource management in South Korea.

Promotion

Promotion is everyone's concern because it provides the sense of personal success, prestige, and increase in monetary and other extrinsic rewards. According to the survey of 590 corporations (366 large corporations and 224 small companies with more than 100 employees by Korean Employers' Federation (1987), promotion to chief clerk (kaychang) from regular staff position takes four years and one month. Promotion to section chief (kwachang) takes three years and one month. It then takes three years and four months to be promoted to deputy manager (chachang) and another three years and one month to be promoted to department manager (puchang). It takes 15.2 years on the average to reach that position after joining an organization as a regular staff member (sawon). The average age of a department manager is 44.7 years old.

However, there has been a change in this trend of promotion in recent years. In Samsung, for example, it takes almost 20 years to be promoted to the position of a business department manager (which is equivalent to a director in other organizations), or 17 years to a regular department manager. It will take 4 years and 6 months to be promoted to a deputy section chief after anyone joins the company as a staff member, or sawon. It will take another 3 years and 6 months to be promoted to section chief B, and two more years to be promoted to section chief A, a regular section chief in other Korean companies. It will take 4 more years to be promoted to a department manager B, an equivalent position of a deputy manager, or chachang in other companies, and three more years to be promoted to a position of department manager A. It will take another three years to be promoted to a position of a department manager of business (It Takes 17 Years 1992). It is projected that, like Japan, a day will come in the near future when section chiefs are in their forties, department managers in their fifties, and executives in their sixties.

According to the practice of the Korean management system, an employee has tenure all the way up to the position of department manager. After tenure, any department manager must resign from his or her organization and is either reappointed to the position of director (eesah) by the organization or has to resign completely from it. A resigned department manager has to find employment in another organization, start his or her own business, or retire completely from the job market.

Promotion is critically important to Koreans because it proves personal success in the organization. It also enhances family prestige and pride, the unique cultural practice in South Korea.

COMPENSATION

Wages and Salaries

Compensation serves an important function of human resource management simply because it relates to money and other extrinsic rewards of employees. However, wage structure is a complicated mixture in the Korean management system. There are several determinants of wages and salaries: contracted basic wage and salary, various allowances, and bonuses. Basic wage and salary plus various allowances are paid monthly, and a bonus payment is added to this monthly payment every other month, usually five times a year. The bonus payment, in many cases, is equivalent to the same amount as a regular monthly payment. Korean employees are, therefore, paid 17 monthly compensation payments (12 months worth of regular monthly salary plus 5 bonus payments).

In the monthly compensation payment, the basic salary is composed of 65 percent, while various allowances account for 35 percent. One researcher identified that most corporations have a total of 128 kinds of allowances (Worker Compensation 1984). For the monthly compensation package of college professors, for example, more than 20 kinds of allowances are included, and even they cannot recognize every component of the compensation package. However, it is optional for organizations to pay allowances and bonuses, and in times of hardship, organizations can sidestep some of the allowances and bonuses because they are not contracted packages.

The underlying reason behind this complex system of compensation in the Korean management system is to keep basic wage and salary levels low. By practicing optional allowances and bonuses, employers can manipulate the compensation system. Another important reason is to link retirement or resignation payments only to basic wage and salary so that organizations may pay smaller retirement or resignation amounts. However, many organizations recognize that most of the allowances are fixed cost in nature. A cost of living increase payment serves as one typical example of an allowance.

According to the survey of 544 corporations by Korean Employers' Federation (1987), 51.7 percent of them decide wages and salaries through

Table 7.4
Wages and Salaries of First-Year Employees

Education	Monthly Salary (won)
College	
Business	303,779
Engineering	314,172
Technical college	246,172
High school	
Technical	212,145
Business	208,889
All female	158,254
Junior high school	
Male	165,438
Female	129,069

Source: Korean Employers' Federation, 1987.

collective bargaining or informal labor–management negotiations. Another 41.2 percent of them decide through company policy. According to one study, the average bonus is 335 percent of monthly salary per year (41% of Worker Compensation 1987).

Wage and salary differences are based on education, age, and seniority. According to the survey of Korean Employers' Federation (1987), the differences in wages and salaries of the first-year employees are shown in Table 7.4. This survey shows that the salary of technical college graduates is 81.1 percent of that of a college graduate with a business major. The salary of high school male graduates is 69.8 percent (54.4 percent for female graduates) of that of college graduates with a business major.

Since 1988, salaries and wages have increased dramatically. According to a survey of the Ministry of Labor (1992), monthly salaries (including various allowances) of 110 leading corporations for management trainees graduated from college are as shown in Table 7.5.

Wage and salary differences also exist by industry. Based on the survey of the Ministry of Labor (1986), salaries by industry are listed in Table 7.6.

According to the survey of 310 large and small corporations by the Daewoo Economic Research Center (1991), the average annual compensation for employees of large corporations was 13.5 million won ($18,000 at the exchange rate of $1 to 750 won), while that of small business employees was 11 million won ($14,667) in 1991. The compensation

Table 7.5
Salaries of Management Trainees

Salary Range (won)		Corporations
1,200,000-1,300,000	($1,538-$1,667)	2 (1.8%)
1,100,000-1,200,000	($1,410-$1,538)	4 (3.6%)
1,000,000-1,100,000	($1,282-$1,410)	7 (6.4%)
900,000-1,000,000	($1,254-$1,282)	15 (13.6%)
800,000-900,000	($1,026-$1,254)	51 (46.4%)
700,000-800,000	($887 - $1,026)	26 (23.6%)
600,000-700,000	($769 - $887)	5 (4.6%)

Note: The exchange rate is $1 to 780 won.

Table 7.6
Salaries by Industries (Unit: Won)

Industry	Department manager	Deputy Dept. manager	Section chief	Deputy sec. chief
All Industries	637,146	562,064	465,629	379,018
Manufacturing	636,450	560,832	464,914	378,591
Construction	695,394	615,096	540,974	420,355
Mining	587,281	530,400	445,875	359,216

Source: The Ministry of Labor, 1986.

package increased 18.4 percent in large corporations and 14.1 percent in small corporations from that of the previous year.

Song (1984) claims that a relatively equitable distribution of income has existed in South Korea from 1965 to 1982 on the basis of the deciles distribution ratio. If anyone takes successive tenths of the distribution, he or she can obtain the first, second, and so on, up to the tenth decile. The first decile score is the one dividing the lowest 10 percent from the upper 90 percent. Weitzman (1989) attributes this distribution to the bonus system which is practiced in South Korea, Japan, and Taiwan and promotes it, calling it a typical example of profit-sharing capitalism.

Retirement Payment

South Korea has no standard retirement age. College professors, for example, retire at 65 years old, while most employees retire at 55 years

Table 7.7
Retirement Age of Corporations

	1978	1982
Retirement at 55	79.2%	83.6%
Retirement at 53	1.3	3.1
Retirement at 56 - 60	10.4	7.4

Source: Korean Employers' Federation, 1987.

old. Government-run corporations have delayed gradually the retirement age up to 60 years, based on the ranks in organizations.

According to the survey of Korean Employers' Federation (1987), the retirement age of corporations is as shown in Table 7.7. There is no clear distinction between retirement and resignation in the Korean management system as to the calculation of payment. Most organizations set aside one month's salary (basic salary or salary plus bonus) as a retirement or resignation fund each year. For example, if an employee retires or resigns at the end of fifteen years of employment, he or she will receive as a lump sum the amount of fifteen months' salary. The number of months worked is the basis for subsequent retirement or resignation compensation. However, for retiring or resigning employees, some organizations apply a progressive method in deciding the number of years served. Most government-run corporations, for example, are very generous in calculating the employment months for retirement by adding 2.5 to 3.5 months per year to the number of years of employment (*Labor Economy Yearbook* 1983). For example, a manager who retires or resigns after serving the organization for 10 years would have a retirement or resignation payment amounting to the lump sum of 155 months' salary (12 months plus 3.5 months times 10 years), instead of 120 months.

There has been an aggressive movement to raise the retirement age for employees since employers have experienced extensive labor shortage in recent years, which they never anticipated. In addition, since South Koreans live longer (average life expectancy in 1991 was 71.3 years, while it was 55.3 years in 1960), retirement at an early age would create social problems for the retirees unless they find a second job or start their own businesses. The South Korean government made it mandatory that organizations with more than 300 employees must have seniors who are over 55 years old and that seniors must comprise at least 3 percent of their work force (It Is Mandatory 1992).

Table 7.8
Fringe Benefits

Programs	Participating companies
Company cafeteria	93.1%
Lunch provided by company	73.9
Work uniforms provided by company	94.3
Company commuting bus service	64.5
Financial support for commuting	25.3
Company built employee apartments	26.1
Financial support for house purchasing	11.2
Company dormitory	42.9
Financial support for employee home improvement	7.5
Health service with company doctor	10.8
Nursing office with company nurses	33.4
Company hospital	12.0
Bath - shower facility	84.8
Company beauty salon	7.8
Library	44.7
Movie - music facility	10.0
Gymnasium and sporting facility	47.8
On-the-job and off-the-job training	71.1
Evening schools	25.4
Cooperatives for employees	35.4
Employee stock option support	19.4
Legal retirement payment	95.0

Source: *Labor Economics Yearbook*, 1987.

Fringe Benefits

Most corporations in South Korea extensively implement fringe benefits for their employees. Kia Group, for example, established a 5.66 billion won ($7.547 million at the exchange rate of $1 to 750 won) employee well-being fund in 1986. Through this fund, the company supports employees by helping them purchase houses or apartments, buy company stocks, support tuition for children of employees, and establish finance cooperatives.

Table 7.8 shows the scope of fringe benefits and participating corporations in 1986. Most Korean organizations strongly support financially their employees who pursue further education from junior high school to doctoral programs. These organizations also support financial aid for tuition for the children of employees. Since home ownership or condominium ownership by employees is a critical problem, many large corporations provide financial support. It will be concluded that the fringe benefits of the Korean management system are very generous.

LABOR–MANAGEMENT RELATIONS

Labor Unions

A satisfactory relationship between labor and management is a pre-requisite for increased labor productivity and maintenance of competitiveness. This implies that the rights of workers must be observed, guaranteed, and respected. Unfortunately, this was not true of past labor–management relationships in South Korea. At that time, the government took a firm policy to suppress the rights of workers and the union movement. Many workers and leaders of the labor movement suffered for their endeavors to organize and maintain labor unions in the Korean management system, despite basic labor laws, such as the Labor Union Act, the Labor–Management Conference Act, and the Labor Standard Act, designed to protect the workers. These laws have never been enforced vigorously nor applied to protect the interests of management at the expense of the workers. The Special Law for National Security of 1971, for example, prohibits unions from getting involved in politics and makes organizing unions very difficult (Shin 1984).

This practice was based on the basic government policy of growth first and distribution later. Workers were deprived of their rights to strike against management, and they had to accept very low wages for long hours of work. Worker dissatisfaction resulted in violent labor strife after the June uprising in 1987. The strife in turn led to the change in government. As of September 31, 1987, 3,480 labor strifes erupted in South Korea. Of these, 3,356 of them occurred after the June uprising. Fortunately, 99.5 percent of them were settled (The Ministry of Labor 1987).

Workers demanded wage and salary increases and claimed that the time had come to share equitably the benefit of economic growth in South Korea. At the same time, workers demanded that managers treat them as worthwhile human beings, while they implemented other improvements in working conditions. This was documented by the survey of 394 corporations of the Korean Employers' Federation (1987), in which 50.4 percent of workers in large corporations and 51.5 percent of small corporations demanded wage increases. The workers' next demand was the improvement of working conditions, including the right to organize unions in their organizations.

The aftermath of the labor strife proved very positive. Many corporation executives have recognized that the days of coexistence between labor and management has arrived and have emphasized cooperative relations, companionship relations, and improved human relations between the two parties. The government has also changed its policy considerably toward labor unions and workers since the June uprising of 1987 by granting much freedom in their labor activities.

Labor unions, however, became stronger and more confrontational for several years after the June uprising of 1987. Some (Darlin 1989, 1990) were concerned about the future of the South Korean economy. However, this unstable situation of labor strife turned around. Corporations and their workers put aside differences to regain ground lost in the late 1980s (Nakarmi and Neff 1990) and predicted a brighter future.

We should all understand the confrontation between labor and management and the subsequent compromise in the context of behavioral patterns of Koreans. Koreans are traditionally confrontational and exhibit extreme behavior, but they calculate cunningly the acceptable limit of their behavior. They reach all the way to the wall, but never break it. They never break their preserved system; instead, they try to reform it. With all the turmoil in South Korea in recent history, casualties have been relatively minor compared with those of other countries. Koreans hate bloodshed, and this will be discussed extensively later in the book.

The South Korean society is also an orderly society. People know their exact position and expected behavior in the society, although their behavior was clouded and confused in times of turmoil. Eventually, Koreans restore social order through painful trial and error. It is amazing, for example, to see that violent unions moderated wage demands that earlier would have seemed nonnegotiable.

According to the report of the Ministry of Labor (1991), the labor union movement was stabilized and showed a decline in union membership, as Table 7.9 indicates. This signifies that the labor movement in the Korean management system laid a sound foundation, and that as a result, violent labor strife will decline considerably. Both management and unions understand precisely that they need each other for their mutual benefit, and they will apply only rational and legal approaches in settling their differences. Both parties finally acknowledge their proper positions in society and will act accordingly in their proper positions.

Working Conditions

South Korean workers work long hours each day. The working hours per week for manufacturing workers were 54.3 in 1984, accounting for the longest in the world. However, working hours decreased to 48.2 hours in the first quarter of 1991 (Trend of Labor 1991). Most manufacturing workers and managers work Monday through Saturday and accept working overtime as a matter of fact. As mentioned before, the number of corporations that practice five days a week or every other Saturday is increasing.

This trend of reducing work hours for Korean workers signifies that

Table 7.9
Labor Unions and Membership

	1987*	1987**	1988	1989	1990
Labor unions	2,742	4,103	6,164	7,883	7,698
Increase/decrease	+67	+1,361	+2,061	+1,719	-185
Changes	+2.5%	+49.6%	+50.2%	+27.9%	-2.35%
Union members (million)	1.050	1.267	1.707	1.942	1.887
Increase/decrease	+14,311	+217,256	+439,999	+224,959	-45,528
Changes	+1.4%	+20.7%	+34.7%	+13.2%	-2.36%
Average member per union	383	309	277	245	245

Source: The Ministry of Labor, 1991.
Note: Figures of 1987* show those of June 1987, while those of 1987** show December
   1987. This compares the labor movement before and after the June Revolution of 1987.
   All the figures of 1988, 1989, and 1990 are those of December of each year. Figures and
   change rates indicate the comparison with the previous year.

Table 7.10
Occupational Accidents

	Total	Deaths	Injuries	Disabilities	Occupational diseases	Rate
1989	134,127	1,724	130,842	25,536	1,561	2.01%
1990	132,893	2,236	129,019	27,813	1,638	1.76
Change	-1,234	+512	-1,823	+2,277	+77	
(%)	-.92	+29.7	-1.39	+8.92	+4.93	-.25

Source: Analysis of Occupational Accidents (1991), the Ministry of Labor.

the Korean management system has shown some signs of transferring
from work ethics to leisure ethics. Many workers now prefer to have
leisure time rather than more money. This preference represents a significant departure from the workers' attitude of the 1960s and 1970s.

Workers in South Korea are concerned about work related injuries,
diseases, and fatalities as do workers in other countries. According to
the report of the Ministry of Labor (1991), occupational accidents occurred
as recorded in Table 7.10. In 1990, 673 construction workers died through
occupational accidents, followed by 626 in manufacturing, 390 in min-
ing, 338 in transportation and communication, 8 in electricity, gas, and
water, and 201 in other industries. Death from these occupational accidents represented an estimated loss of 2.7 trillion won ($3.6 billion at
the exchange rate of $1 to 750 won).

Layoffs

Whenever corporations and other nonbusiness organizations have hardships and are obliged to reduce the work force, they implement a layoff process, and most South Korean workers and managers accept this as a matter of fact. When the economy turned sour in 1985, corporations with more than ten employees laid off a total of 80,000 workers and managers (Recession Resulted in Layoffs 1985). The shipping industry is another example. For the three months, January through March 1987, the industry laid off 3,600 employees (Shipbuilding Industry Layoffs 1987). Pungsan Metals, a defense industry company, also laid off 1,140 throughout 1990 (Pungsan Layoffs 1990).

Employee layoffs are not confined to low-level workers. Whenever corporations are affected, they lay off not only manufacturing workers, but also mid-level managers. When South Korea experienced an economic downturn in 1985, some of the publicly listed corporations laid off 173 managers and top executives, claiming that layoffs were an unavoidable practice in unfavorable situations or recessions (Recession Resulted in Layoffs 1985).

The layoffs of 200 mid-level managers of Daewoo Group was already mentioned. In the first half of 1992, Hankuk Yuri, a giant glass manufacturer, laid off more than 200 employees, including upper-level managers, and Daewoo Electronics was scheduled to reduce its number of employees to 12,000 in 1992 from 16,000 in 1988 (Lee 1992).

Labor Turnover

In the Korean management system, employees change their jobs freely, although many of them remain in the same organization until they retire, implying that the turnover rate is relatively high. According to the survey of 1,500 employees of 318 large and small corporations by International Labor Organization and Economic Research Center of Seoul National University (1977), 47.8 percent responded "yes" to the question, "Will you change your job if you are offered 20 percent more salary by other companies?" Employees in South Korea weighed their personal interests and loyalty to their organizations and changed their work places when their personal interests outweighed their loyalty to their current employer.

Another example clearly demonstrates a turnover case. A vice president resigned from Korea Electric Public Corporation in 1977 after he was offered a job as the president of an engineering company. Not only did he take the job; he then persuaded all of the subordinates in his department to change their jobs to the engineering company. We can explain this phenomenon by the unique feature of the Korean manage-

Table 7.11
Reasons for Turnover

Contract expired	Retirement	Layoffs	Discharges	Occupational accidents	Employee initiated
1,986	3,504	2,623	7,724	7,086	615,255
.3%	.5%	.4%	1.2%	1.1&	96.4%

Source: The Ministry of Labor, 1986.
Note: The statistics are as of the first half of 1986.

ment system that Korean people are individualistic and group-oriented at the same time.

Table 7.11 shows the major reasons for the turnover in the Korean management system. There were many reasons for employee-initiated turnover. Women employees dropped from the job market completely for marriage, and other employees became full-time students, or simply changed their jobs.

Labor Laws

Many labor laws regulate labor–management relations. The Labor Standard Act is the basic labor law in South Korea. According to this law, corporations are obliged to provide the work procedure that must meet the approval of the Department of Labor. The Labor Union Act guarantees the right to organize unions with 30 charter members. More than half the workers must approve of the union.

The Labor Strife Act, the Labor Committee Act, and the Labor–Management Conference Act are other important labor laws. If a company fires an employee, the process must have the approval of the Labor Committee according to the Labor Committee Act. There is also the Occupational Safety and Health Act to protect workers from occupational injuries and unsafe working conditions. For example, the Occupational Injuries Compensation Act deals with compensation for work related injuries. The Minimum Wage Act regulates the minimum compensation for workers. Recently, the government tried to revise existing labor laws in order to maintain peaceful coexistence between labor and management.

CONCLUSIONS

The practice of human resource management in the Korean management system has some unique features that we cannot readily identify in other countries due to the unique characteristics of the Korean people and their culture. There are strengths and weaknesses in this practice, but no one can deny that South Korea's impressive economic growth is attributed significantly to the effective use of human resources. In this chapter, all of the areas of human resource management were discussed in the context of characteristics of the Korean management system, and we admit that there are still many problem areas. However, when we interviewed several managers, we realized their determination in correcting such problems and agree that further study is needed for the better understanding of human resource management in South Korea.

In the next chapter, the human resource management of a company in South Korea will be discussed. Although the practice of this company may not deviate significantly from the general practice of human resource management in South Korea, it is in our interests to see how individual companies practice human resource management in their organizations.

REFERENCES

A Survey of Job Situations. Seoul: The Human Resource Bank of Korean Employers' Federation, 1987.

A Survey of Labor Strife. Seoul: The Ministry of Labor, 1987.

A Survey on Labor Turnover of Employees. Seoul: The Economic Research Center of Seoul National University, 1977.

A Survey of Salaries of Entering Management Trainees. Seoul: The Ministry of Labor, 1992.

The Bank of Korea. The Preliminary Statistics of the Economy of 1991. Seoul: The Bank of Korea, 1992.

Chang, C. S. Chaebol: The South Korean Conglomerates. Business Horizons (March-April, 1988).

Colleges Worry about Job Market. The Dong-A Daily News (September 25, 1986).

Darlin, D. Korea's Unions, Suppressed for Decades, Become Stronger, More Confrontational. The Wall Street Journal (April 12, 1989).

———. South Korean Labor Peace is Shattered. The Wall Street Journal (May 2, 1990).

Discrepancy of Compensation between Large and Small Companies. Seoul: The Daewoo Economic Research Center, 1991.

Hong, K. D. 41% of Compensation Decided without Labor–Management Agreement. The Dong-A Daily News (August 21, 1987).

It Is Mandatory to Hire Workers Over 55 Years Old. The Hankuk Daily News (June 11, 1992).

It Takes almost 17 Years to be Promoted to Department Manager at Samsung. The Hankuk Daily News (September 22, 1992).

Korean Employers' Federation, 1987.

Labor Economy Yearbook (in Korean), 1983.

Lee, K. U. Endless Efforts to Make it Lean. The Hankuk Daily News (June 13, 1992).

Male Only Applicants Advertisements Prosecuted for the First Time. *The Dong-A Daily News* (March 27, 1990).

Nakarmi, L. At Daewoo, A "Revolution" at the Top. *Business Week* (February 18, 1991).

——, and Neff, R. Can This Tiger Burn Bright Again? *Business Week* (December 3, 1990).

Personality is an Important Factor Employment for College Graduates. *The Dong-A Daily News* (September 5, 1991).

Pungsan Metals Layoffs Employees. *The Dong-A Daily News* (January 18, 1990).

Recession Resulted in Layoffs. *The Dong-A Daily News* (November 19, 1985).

Salary Discrepancy between Graduates of High Schools and Colleges is 27%. *The Dong-A Daily News* (August 6, 1987).

Shin, Y. K. Human Resource Management in the South Korean Industry. Paper presented at the Korean Human Resource Management Association Convention in Seoul, Korea, 1988.

——. *Hankuk Kiupui Tuksungkwa Kwaje* (Features and Problems of Korean Corporations). Seoul: Seoul National University Press, 1984.

Shipbuilding Industry Layoffs Workers. *The Dong-A Daily News* (June 9, 1987).

Song, B. R. *The Korean Economy* (in Korean). Seoul: Parkyongsa, 1984.

South Korea's Wage Guidelines. *The Wall Street Journal* (December 10, 1990).

Trend of Labor Movement. The Korea Labor Research Center, 1991.

Weitzman, M. L. Profit-sharing Capitalism. In J. Elster and K. O. Moene (eds.), *Alternative to Capitalism,* pp. 61–70. Cambridge: Cambridge University Press, 1989.

Worker Compensation Decided by Owner-Managers. *The Dong-A Daily News* (December 4, 1984).

Yang, B. M., and Park, S. J. Lectures on the Seminar of Problems with the Wage System and an Alternative Approach to Improve, 1991.

Yonsei Medical Center News, no. 129 (June 22, 1987).

8

Human Resource Management of Ottogi Foods Industrial Co. Ltd.: A Case Study

Ottogi Foods Co., Ltd., near Seoul, South Korea, was established in 1969. It produces powdered curry, tomato catchup, mayonnaise, pepper, vinegar, and other food and food-related goods. In 1987, the company had nearly 2,000 employees, and sales reached 80 billion won ($100 million, at the exchange rate of $1 to 800 won) (Kim 1988). The company is not as large as a *chaebol* group corporation in South Korea, but it has a reputation of being a well-managed company. This case study was conducted in June 1987, in Seoul, Korea.

ORGANIZATION OF THE COMPANY

The organizational structure of Ottogi Foods is similar to that of other Korean corporations, and the hierarchical structure of it is conducive to the Korean management system. The company has not adopted the system of chairman and vice president. Instead, there are two categories of employees: tenured and nontenured. After a probationary period, employees become tenured; the same rule applies to up to the department manager, or puchang. From the position of director, eesah, and up, the managers of the company become nontenured employees and are reappointed every three years. If they fail to be reappointed, they must leave the company or be assigned to an equivalent or lesser position at one of the sister companies.

There are five departments in the company: Personnel, Finance, Production, Marketing, and Research Center. The offices of Managing

Figure 8.1
Ottogi Foods Organizational Structure

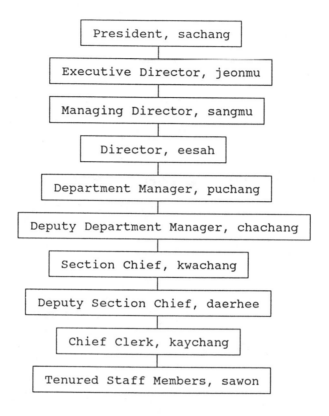

Inspector, or kamsa, and Strategic Planning are performing staff functions. The Personnel Department oversees three areas of related business: general business of the company, personnel, and reserve army related business.

RECRUITING AND SELECTING

Recruiting

Based on manpower planning, the company prepares its recruiting strategy in July for the upcoming year. Each department submits its manpower planning to the Personnel Department, and the president makes the final decision for needed manpower. By November, all the planning for recruiting and selecting for the coming year is complete.

The company has adopted an open recruitment system through various channels—morning and evening newspapers, and recommendations from teachers or professors—and it advertises for recruitment once a year in these newspapers. Recommendations of teachers or professors are used on a limited basis. The company begins recruiting after the chaebol group corporations have completed their recruitment because the company cannot compete with giant corporations for recruits. Since chaebol corporations recruit uniformly during the first part of November each year, the company recruits early each year.

In 1984, five times the number of recruits applied for each position, and 5,500 applied for 74 positions in 1986, many applicants preferring positions in general business. Positions in the sales force were not as popular as general business positions, and few recruits applied for positions in the Research Center.

The company requires each applicant to submit the following documents: a resume, school transcripts, a copy of a citizenship card, a photo, a proof of completion of military duty for male applicants, and a copy of a license, if applicable.

Selecting

The selection process is administered by the Selection Committee, and there are several stages of it. In the first stage, applicants numbering five or six times the number of job positions available are evaluated on the basis of criteria, which include school grades, completion of military duty for male applicants, photo evaluation, and the applicant's family background. The selection committee prefers those applicants whose school grades average a "B" or better with a good family background. Next, the successful applicants complete the company application form and take a 90-minute written test of English and their major concentration area. Some are required to take dexterity tests. A week after the tests, applicants numbering only two or three times the number of available positions are notified of their successful performance. Four or five days later, these candidates are interviewed. The interview is conducted by the president, executive director, the personnel manager, and the respective department manager as a group, and is based on the following issues: the reason that the applicant applied to the company, job experience or training, family background, attitudes of the applicant, and his or her health condition.

After the interview, the applicant selection is finalized when the company personnel director informs him or her two days later of the results of the interviews. Four or five days later, the successful applicants return to the company to take a physical examination and to file more documents for company records. Seven to ten days after the successful physical examination, the final notification of employment is issued to the applicants. The selection process is now completed. In 1986, 74 out of 5,500 applicants were employed by the company.

Orientation

The company's orientation program is integrated with the three-month probation period in which each management trainee receives 90 percent of the contract salary. During the orientation program, lasting seven weeks to three months, department managers explain company policies and procedures, and top executives lecture on moral issues. Perhaps two or three outside lecturers are invited for the orientation. New management trainees then spend time together for one week at the Canaan Farmer's School for physical and mental preparedness. They also learn the company procedures through apprentice practice. After the orientation, they are assigned to their permanent positions in the company.

TRAINING AND DEVELOPMENT

The company conducts on-the-job training for the employees. For training in the Marketing Department, outside lecturers lead instructional programs once or twice a year. The sales force provides lecture programs four times a year. For manufacturing workers, the department conducts moral education and quality control programs. Learning foreign languages, such as English and Japanese, comprises an important part of the training program. Most managers are required to take a one-year foreign language course by studying one and a half hours every working day before or after working hours.

For off-the-job training, the company sends managers and engineers to companies in Japan, which have technical relationships with them. They stay in Japan from nine months to one year, and the company pays all of the expenses for this training. Once an employee has two or more years of company service, the company also reimburses all expenses for the tuition of an employee who pursues an advanced degree in evening classes. Thus, training and development is an important program for the company.

EVALUATION AND PROMOTION

The employee evaluation process is conducted twice a year. Superiors in the company evaluate their subordinates by filling out one of four types of evaluation formats: one for general staff, another for the sales force, the third for production workers, and the fourth for marketing employees. These are similar in nature to the ones used in the United States.

The evaluation format for general staff contains three broad subjects for evaluation: performance, capability, and attitudes. In the performance section, staff members are evaluated on their performance quality, quantity, and improvement. Capability evaluation assesses employee job knowledge, planning capacity, judgment, sociability, pursuance, and communication skills. In the section on attitude, employees are evaluated on their sense of responsibility, assertiveness, cooperation, diligence, and personal behaviors.

Each criterion is arranged with a ranking scale of five points, except for both performance quality and pursuance, which have eight points each. In addition, employee's health is evaluated on the basis of five points. Consistent attendance deserves 10 points; for each absence from work, 1 point is deducted, and 0.3 points is deducted for each tardiness or early leave from work. Altogether, the evaluation format totals 100 points.

Each employee is evaluated by two superiors. For regular staff members, their section chief and chief clerk evaluate them. In turn, the section chief and department manager evaluate chief clerks, and section chiefs are evaluated by their department manager and related director. Finally, department managers are evaluated by the managing director and the president. There is no formal evaluation process for nontenured executives. The president and the executive director evaluate them informally based on their performance and leadership.

There is no conference between evaluators and those being evaluated. The latter are not informed officially on the outcome of the evaluation process, and the employees usually do not exercise their right to access the outcome of the evaluation. The evaluation process is not the highest priority for employees because the seniority system is as important as the evaluation process.

Evaluation is still important because it relates closely to promotion and the increase in extrinsic rewards. However, this evaluation–promotion connection conflicts with the seniority system in the Korean management system. The company observes the seniority system that links an employee's promotion directly to the number of years he or she has served. For example, it takes three years for college graduates, four years for technical college graduates, and five years for high school graduates, to be promoted to the rank of chief clerk after employees join the company. Regardless of education, it takes another two years to advance to the rank of deputy section chief from chief clerk. Two more years are needed for an employee to be promoted to the rank of section chief from deputy section chief, and another two years are required to be promoted to the rank of deputy manager. Employees will become department managers, the highest tenured position, after serving more than three years as deputy managers. This promotion process is almost semiautomatic under the seniority system unless the formal evaluation significantly damages any employee.

Once an employee is qualified for promotion, his superior recommends him, and the Executive Committee decides upon his promotion. The committee is composed of the president, the executive director, the respective department manager, and the director of the Planning Board. Those candidates who have been awarded prizes, who have never been absent from work, who have never been punished, and who have been working long and hard are likely to be promoted. As in most other companies in South Korea, this company does not promote female employees to the position of manager.

COMPENSATION

Compensation is an important part of any organization's makeup because it directly affects the livelihood and prestige of employees. Employee compensation is composed of wages and salaries with various allowances and bonuses, fringe benefits, and retirement and resignation payments. Wages are the compensation for hourly wage workers, and salaries are the compensation for monthly paid workers and managers. After reviewing the wages and salaries at six or seven other food processing companies, the company decides upon the wages and salaries of the company employees by setting the range a little above the average of the compensations of these companies. The salaries of first-year employees of the company in 1987 were as shown in Table 8.1.

As in other companies in South Korea, this company discriminates against female workers and managers in terms of compensation. Female employees with college degrees, for example, earn 77.46 percent of the salary of their male counterparts, and those with high school diplomas earn 72.54 percent of the salary of their male counterparts. The monthly salary of male high school graduates is 68.73 percent of that of male college graduates. An employee's education is, therefore, an important factor in determining his or her salary. Salaries of the company managers in 1987 were as shown in Table 8.2.

In the four grade levels for each rank, Grade 3 is the highest, followed by Grade 2A and Grade 2B. Grade 1 is the lowest grade level. The salary of employees of the same rank will differ on the basis of the employee's grade. The company's compensation is higher than the national average of all industries. Salaries of employees increased 5 to 10 percent annually until the June uprising of 1987 and are the sum of the basic contract amount and various monthly allowances, such as a cost of living allowance, a sales allowance, and a job allowance.

The company also pays a bonus three times a year: in the summer, the fall, and at the end of the year. An employee's annual bonuses amount

Table 8.1
Monthly Salary of First-Year Employees

Employees	Monthly Salaries (won)
College graduates (Male)	355,000 (100.00%)
College graduates (Female)	275,000 (77.46%)
Technical college graduates (Male)	279,000 (78.59%)
Technical college graduates (Female)	200,000 (56.34%)
High school graduates (Male)	244,000 (68.73%)
High school graduates (Female)	177,000 (49.86%)

Source: The Personnel Department of Ottogi Foods Industrial Co. Ltd., June 1987.
Note: The salary of 355,000 won is approximately $449 at $1 to 780 won.

Table 8.2
Salary of Company Managers

Managers	Monthly Salaries (won)
Chief clerk	429,000
Deputy section chief	525,000
Section chief	625,000
Deputy manager	725,000
Department manager	825,000
Director	1,100,000–1,300,000

Source: The Personnel Department of Ottogi Foods Industrial Co. Ltd., June 1987.
Note: The salary of 1,300,000 won is $1,667 at $1 to 780 won.

to 400 percent of his or her monthly basic salary plus allowances. Other companies pay bonuses of up to 300 to 600 percent of the monthly salary each year. The monthly compensation of section chief of the company, for example, is not 625,000 won: Instead, it actually amounts to 833,333 won (625,000 won + [625,000 × 400% /12]).

Tenured employees retire at age 55. One month's salary (basic salary plus bonus) is put aside by the company each year for each employee as the resource fund for retirement or resignation. If an employee retires or resigns after 20 years of service, he or she receives the amount of 20 months' salary as a retirement or resignation payment. For example, a department manager receives 17,708,320 won ($22,703 at the exchange rate of $1 to 780 won) as a retirement or resignation payment. The company pays this lump sum two weeks after the employee retires or resigns from the company.

There is no specific retirement age for nontenured managers, although they usually retire at age 60. If a department manager is promoted to director, he must formally resign from his position as department manager and be reappointed simultaneously by the company. This means that he receives his resignation payment at the same time that he is promoted to the position of director, a nontenured position. His number of years of service starts all over again in counting years of service for retirement or resignation payment.

FRINGE BENEFITS

The company distributes 100 shares of stock each year to those regular staff members with ten years of employment and to those managers above the rank of chief clerk with three years of employment. The company also contributes to employee health insurance, paying 2 percent of employees' salaries to the insurance system. This amount will cover 30 to 50 percent of health expenses. Each employee also contributes 2 percent of his or her salary.

The company provides five buses for commuting employees and also serves them free lunch, prepared by an employed dietician. The employees have a one-hour lunch in which all the workers and managers, including the president of the company, eat together in the company cafeteria. The company also has recreational facilities such as a swimming pool, tennis courts, and a basketball court for its employees.

The company observes paid holidays and vacations in compliance with the Labor Standard Act. There are five national holidays and a Labor Day holiday. Each month, employees are entitled to set aside one day as a vacation day. In addition, on an annual basis, at the end of the first year of employment, they have the right to claim eight vacation days, and one day is added for each year's service after the second year of employment. Therefore, at the end of the first year, employees have altogether 26 days of holidays and vacations (6 national holidays + 12 monthly vacation days + 8 vacation days). If employees work on holidays, they receive 250 percent of a working day's salary: 100 percent as regular pay and 150 percent as holiday compensation. Employees receive 200 percent of a day's salary if they work on vacation days: 100 percent each as regular and vacation compensations. Many company employees prefer working on holidays and vacation days rather than enjoying them mainly because of additional monetary rewards.

LABOR–MANAGEMENT RELATIONS

A labor union was organized in 1985 without notifying the company, but it later recognized the union as the official union, belonging to the

Union of Chemical Industry. The union has approximately 700 members out of almost 2,000 employees, and most of them are manufacturing workers. The Labor Union Act prohibits managers above the rank of chief clerk to join unions. Union members pay 1 percent of their wages or salaries as membership dues.

In the Ottogi Foods Company, both the union and the company are represented by five representatives each. The president, the personnel manager, the director (eesah) for manufacturing, the director of marketing, and production department manager represent the company. The president of the labor union and four other top union leaders represent the workers. The following is the agenda of the conference:

1. Increasing both worker productivity and the well-being of the workers,
2. Training of workers,
3. Preventive measures for labor strife,
4. Grievances of workers,
5. Safety, health, and improvement of working conditions of workers, and
6. Other items involving cooperation between labor and management.

Some workers complained about their inhumane treatment by managers; more specifically, workers are very sensitive to the insulting attitudes of some managers. Some female manufacturing workers complained about their low wages. For a long time, the company had experienced no labor strife; however, there were 3,480 reported incidents after the June uprising of 1987 in South Korea.

LABOR TURNOVER

Table 8.3 shows the turnover rate of the company in 1986. The company personnel manager informed us that the turnover rate was 21.3 percent in 1986. Female wage workers accounted for up to 70 percent of the resignations among employees resigning with two years of service, and female workers' turnover rate was very high. The turnover rate of managers was 10.2 percent.

Table 8.4 outlines the reasons for employees' resignation from the company in 1986. This data verifies that Korean employees feel free to change their jobs if necessary, and they occasionally take the initiative for such action.

CONCLUSIONS

Since this case study, the company has grown into an organization with more than 3,000 employees. Since 1987, the salary of employees

Table 8.3
Turnover Rate

Years of Employment	Number of Resignation
6 months or less	40 (27.2%)
6 months - 1 year	16 (10.8%)
1 - 2 years	24 (16.3%)
2 - 3 years	18 (12.2%)
3 - 4 years	16 (10.8%)
4 - 5 years	16 (10.8%)
5 - 6 years	4 (2.7%)
6 - 7 years	2 (1.3%)
7 years and over	11 (7.4%)
Total	147 (100%)

Source: The Personnel Department of Ottogi Foods Industrial Co. Ltd., June 1987.

Table 8.4
Reasons for Resignation

Reasons for Resignation	Total	Male	Female
Changing jobs	18	12	6
Marriage	19	–	19
Returning to school	2	–	2
Illness	18	4	14
Absences without notification	19	3	16
Returning to hometown	9	1	8
Opening new business	11	9	2
Problems with aptitude capacity	17	8	9
Forced resignation	18	4	14
Staying home	7	2	5
Others	9	4	5
Total	147	47	100

Source: The Personnel Department of Ottogi Foods Industrial Co. Ltd., June 1987.

increased by double digits each year until recently. The brand name, Ottogi, is now a household word in South Korea, and Oriental grocery stores in the United States sell many company products. In addition, the company has extended its business multinationally to include the Eastern European countries.

Human resource management at Ottogi Foods is a typical example of the Korean management system. The phenomenal growth of the company can be attributed, in part, to the effective utilization of human resource management there. Effective, determined, and creative leadership is another factor that contributed to this growth.

In the next chapter, we will extensively review the Office of Planning and Control of corporations, the think tanks of their organizations. Many corporations including chaebol groups owe them much for obtaining new, and sometimes secret, information. Corporations also owe them much for the establishment of merging and acquisition strategies and for the development of new products.

REFERENCES

Kim, K. M. The collapse of Chungbo Food of Many Gossips (in Korean). *The Shin Dong-A* (January, 1988).

9

Office of Planning and Control: Think Tanks of Organizations

You may wonder how the chairmen of *chaebol* groups are able to manage so many corporations. Most founders of chaebol groups and other corporations are paternalistic and autocratic managers. However, their management styles are somewhat different, based on their personalities, value systems, and perceptions. In general, there are three types of management styles used by top corporate executives: (1) the Physical Inventory Method, (2) the Perpetual Inventory Method, and (3) the Profit Centers style.

The Physical Inventory Method of management involves founders or top executives who intervene in almost every aspect of their organizations. Daily, they confront managers and workers to ask questions, to give orders, to control their operations, and to make sure that their employees perform their jobs enthusiastically and effectively. They are not satisfied being confined to their offices, managing by telephone, or summoning subordinates to their offices; they must see and evaluate their organizations themselves. They are managers with stamina and energy, and they demand their subordinates to fulfill their assigned jobs. Chung Ju Yong, the founder of Hyundai Group, was a typical manager who used the management style of the physical inventory method (Bae 1985).

Other chairmen or top executives use the management style of perpetual inventory method. These executives manage their organizations, based on information provided by key assistants. Without leaving their offices, they know the status of the organization and about the performance of their subordinates. There is no physical confrontation with their employees. This management style can be effective only when the information obtained is accurate and timely. The late Lee Bung Chull, founder of Samsung Group, used this management style.

There is a third type of management style in the Korean management system, the Profit Centers style. This management style delegates authority to individual managers as long as they perform their duties effectively and profitably. Some top executives, mostly the second generation of the corporation founders, strictly apply the concept of profit centers style. The delegation of authority to individual corporations in the group is based on the information provided by a group of subordinates in the head office who, in turn, obtain information from assistants in individual corporations. Unlike most executives of the first two types, these top executives are college educated, some of them having earned advanced degrees, mostly from the United States. Even though they can be classified as paternalistic and autocratic by Korean standards, their management style is similar to the "System 3 Management" of Rensis Likert (Likert 1961). Kim Suk Won, chairman of Ssangyong Group, a second generation executive, is a typical example of a profit center manager.

These three management styles have proven to be very effective, although each of them has received much criticism. However, they have one thing in common: Founders of chaebol groups and other top executives apply in their organizations one of the three management styles based on the information furnished by the office of planning and control, or think tanks. For the first two management styles, think tanks are organized in the head office, called "kihwoik jochong sil" in the Korean management system.

A typical office of planning and control functions as the nerve center of the entire organization. However, the third management style has rather decentralized think tank groups: One is in the head office, and others are in individual corporations in the group. The central and peripheral think tanks coordinate to provide relevant information to executives both at the head office and in individual corporations.

Some South Korean managers call think tanks the "problem solvers" for their organizations. It is, therefore, very important to understand the nature of the think tanks in the Korean management system. Think-tank groups are groups of capable people who provide sound advice to executives on the basis of reliable and relevant information. Usually experienced, talented, and well educated, they are the elite employees of their organizations.

The main objectives of think tanks are to provide relevant and valuable information for the decision-making process to top executives, to formalize long-range strategic planing, to monitor finance and personnel, and to consolidate diversified corporations into one chaebol or organization. They propose blueprints for future product lines, critically analyze the impact of changes in domestic and international environments on their enterprises, and recommend strategies to deal with such volatile environments. They use their research to identify available capital funds in both domestic and international financial markets. They also set the priorities for various investments.

The Office of Planning and Control of Samsung Group, for example, is the oldest and one of the largest think tanks of any corporation in South Korea. This office began with approximately 20 staff members in 1956, but the office has expanded to employ more than 200 staff members working in 13 teams in 1987 (Kim 1988). Each team consists of a secretary and members of the following departments: Operations, Business Finance, International Finance, Planning, Personnel, Computer, Auditing, Quality Control, Technology Control, Business Information, North and South American Operations, and Public Relations. Another three teams monitor the operations of the group. One of the operation teams deals with electronics; the second team concentrates on manufacturing; and the third group specializes in heavy industry. These three teams carefully monitor the business operations of individual corporations of the group and set priorities for investments for the corporations of the group.

Samsung's Office of Planning and Control is organized under a group of five managing directors (sangmu), and six directors (eesah). The importance of the office was emphasized by Lee Byung Chull, the late chairman, when he stated, "Without the Office of Planning and Control, there will be no Samsung" (Kim 1988, p. 559). Since the office is critically important to the chairman and Samsung Group as a whole, the most capable and trustworthy managers are assigned as directors of the office. This practice applies to all the chaebol groups and other corporations.

Hyundai Group refers to its think tank as "the Office of Comprehensive Planning," which was established in January 1979 (Kim 1988). Under the director of the office, there is one vice director who has the rank of managing director. There are two directors.

The organization has four teams on finance, two teams on personnel, and a bureau of human resource development. Team 1 on finance deals with tax and exporting, team 2 handles bank finances, team 3 evaluates the performance of individual corporations within the group, and team 4 evaluates the priority of new investments. Personnel Team 1 deals with the planning of human resource management for the group, and team 2, established after the Hyundai Group experienced severe labor strife in 1987, oversees labor–management relations.

Lucky–Goldstar Group also has an Office of Planning, which acts as a think-tank group. This group has more than 150 staff members of which 80 percent are managers above the rank of section chief, or kwachang (Kim 1988). The Office of Planning looks like an independent corporation in the group because there is a president (sachang), two vice presidents (pusachang), two executive directors (jeonmu), three managing directors (sangmu), and four directors (eesah). The office hierarchy comprises one staff section and nine teams, and the head of each team has the rank of department manager (puchang).

The office was established in January 1968. The first director was the son-in-law of the uncle of the founder of Lucky–Goldstar Group. In 1987, the office recommended a reorganization of the entire office into three broad subgroups. One subgroup was to deal with chemicals and energy, another was to concentrate on electronics and communication, and the third was to cover finance and services.

The Office of Planning and Control of Daewoo Group is one of the largest and most effective organizations among chaebol group corporations (Kim 1988). Kim Woo Choong, the chairman of the group, depends heavily on the information and recommendations for his decision-making process.

According to the Daewoo telephone directory (as of June 1, 1989), there were 21 upper-level managers and 60 middle-level managers from the rank of department manager (puchang), to section chief (kwachang) in the Office of Planning and Control. The office was organized as follows:

Vice President	1
Executive Director	5
Managing Director	7
Director	1
Director appointed Department Manager	7

Under their supervision, the following 12 departments and sections function in the office:

Manpower Planning Section 1	Department Manager	1
	Section Chief	3
Training and Development	Deputy Dept. Manager	4
	Section Chief	5
Manpower Planning Section 2	Department Manager	1
	Deputy Dept. Manager	2
	Section Chief	1
Total Quality Control	Department Manager	1
	Section Chief	1
Public Relations	Section Chief	3
Information Investigation	Department Manager	1
	Section Chief	1
Organizational Culture	Department Manager	1
	Section Chief	1

Managerial Control	Deputy Dept. Manager	1
	Section Chief	2
Management Audit	Department Manager	1
	Deputy Dept. Manager	2
	Section Chief	9
C. I. Team	Department Manager	2
	Deputy Dept. Manager	3
	Section Chief	4
Legal Affairs	Department Manager	3
	Deputy Dept. Manager	1
	Section Chief	3
Physical Health/Sports	Section Chief	3

The rank of deputy department manager (chachang), is a position between section chief and department manager.

The Office of Business Planning of Sunkyong Group was established in 1974 (Kim 1988). The office has six managers: one with the rank of president, one with the rank of vice president, three with the rank of managing director (sangmu), and one with the rank of director (eesah). There are 56 staff members in five departments: Personnel, Long-range Strategic Planning, Finance, Marketing, and Secretariat.

An important contribution of this office was the successful implementation of strategy for the takeover of Gulf Corporation of the United States when this corporation decided to withdraw its operation from South Korea. When Sunkyong Group learned of Gulf's withdrawal, the chairman initiated a strategy to take it over on the basis of the initiative and strategy recommendations of the Office of Business Planning. In 1987, the sale of gasoline and oil products accounted for almost one-half of the entire sales of the group.

The function of the Office of Comprehensive Control of Ssangyong Group is unique among think tank groups of chaebol corporations (Kim 1988). Since the chairman of Ssangyong uses the management style of decentralized profit center, there are dual systems for planning and control: The head office has one, and individual corporations of Ssangyong have their own offices for planning and control. The presidents of these corporations have virtual autonomy and authority for managing their corporations. It is crucial to the decision-making process of each president to have access to relevant information provided by his own planning and control offices. As a result, the main function of the staff in the head office is to coordinate the head office with the individual corporations in the group.

The Ssangyong office, established in 1962, has two departments with 25 staff members. One department is called the "Department of Moral Behavior" and concentrates on the promotion of the group's corporate culture and quality control. The other is named the "Department of Business Management," and it oversees medium and long-range planning, operations, new product development, new investments, and information gathering.

Unlike other chaebol group organizations, Hankuk Hwayak Group has two types of offices of planning and control as think-tank groups: the Office of Business Control and the Office of Comprehensive Planning (Kim 1988). The former office, established in 1973, coordinates operations of the corporations in the group and has 60 staff members. Under the director of the office, there are five teams—Personnel, Finance, Audit, Operation, and Material Control—and six executives in the office—one with the rank of vice president (pusachang), three managing directors (sangmu), and two directors (eesah). The Personnel Team concentrates on the human resource management of the entire group, the Finance Team deals with the coordination of budgets of group corporations, and the Audit Team focuses on performance analysis and evaluation. The Operations Team, a very influential office divided into seven subteams, oversees the operations of individual corporations within the group as well as every aspect of the operations of the entire group.

The Office of Comprehensive Planning specializes in long-range planning, information gathering for the domestic and international economy, and in analyzing new investment opportunities for Hankuk Hwayak Group. This office, established in 1966, consists of 35 members including one executive director, and three directors. There are three teams in this office: Information, Planning, and Finance.

The Office of Comprehensive Planning and Control of Hyosung Group was established in 1981, but actually started to operate in 1983 (Kim 1988). The office has 50 members, managed by four executives—one president, one executive director, and two auditors—and nine teams— Secretariat, Moral Consciousness, Public Relations, Personnel, Business Planning, Business Control, Audit, Technology, and Sports. Since 1986, the group has changed in the direction of aggressive expansion, and some of the teams in the office played an important role in affecting this change. More specifically, the Team of Business Planning, which administers medium and long-range planning and finance, the Team of Business Control, which deals with the analysis and evaluation of the performance of individual corporations in the entire group, and the Team of Technology, which concentrates on new investments, have contributed significantly to the growth of the entire group.

Ingenious ideas of chaebol group founders and top executives of organizations are supplemented by the intensive feasibility study by think-tank personnel of the organizations. Or, the unique ideas recommended by think-tank teams are carefully scrutinized by entrepreneurial talents of chaebol group founders and top executives for feasibility of development into commercial values and eventually into profits.

Think-tank group personnel also contribute by bringing their diversified corporate organizations into conformity with their entire organizations. Through their contribution and influence, think-tank personnel are able to gather all their organizations under a giant umbrella of chaebol groups or other non-chaebol group organizations. After having investigated all the opportunities of external environments, they are also able to direct the entire group organization into a productive and meaningful future.

At present, think-tank group personnel of giant corporations are looking forward to the challenging opportunity of opening new markets of Russian Commonwealth Republics and Eastern European countries. They are also investigating the opportunity of opening markets in countries whose economies are based on central planning, such as China, Vietnam, and North Korea. If these think-tank teams develop novel and workable strategies in cultivating these opportunities, South Korea may experience a second leap or miracle for the South Korean economy.

The offices of planning and control of most chaebol groups are desperate to gather accurate and reliable information from the government and from other competing companies for their strategy formulation and implementation in order to survive and prosper. The second mobile transportation project has been the largest venture of the Sixth Republic of the Roh Tae Woo government. In the first-round review and evaluation process of the Department of Postal Service and Transportation, Sunkyong Group earned the highest points for bidding on the project. The difference between Sunkyong Group and Kolon Group, the second highest bidder, was as much as 344 points. All the six major chaebol groups applied for bidding on the project, and their points were far from those of Sunkyong.

Staff members of the Office of Planning and Control of Sunkyong had prepared for this project in complete secrecy by developing the 97 evaluation criteria and licensing guidelines of the Department of Postal Service and Transportation. Through careful analysis, Sunkyong Group identified rather accurately most of the evaluation criteria and the licensing guidelines and later responded to them correctly (*The Weekly Hankuk* 1992).

As mentioned before, Samsung Group has obtained permission from the government to produce commercial vehicles, which was once denied by the government. Through an extensive information network, the staff of the Office of Planning and Control of Samsung had obtained the information that the government intended to implement the free competition principle in granting the right to produce vehicles in South

Korea. Furthermore, they learned that Hyundai, one of the major car producers, did not oppose Samsung's plan to produce vehicles. With this information, Samsung Group aggressively pursued permission to manufacture vehicles and was successful at last in obtaining permission from the government (*The Weekly Hankuk* 1992).

Corporations including chaebol group corporations are keenly aware that obtaining accurate and reliable information from government agencies and competing companies is a sure way to guarantee their survival and prosperity. It is also a sure way to stay ahead of their competitors. These corporations have developed a fine network for gathering information through their offices of planning and control.

CONCLUSIONS

One of the main features of the Korean management system is the combination of entrepreneurial talents of corporation founders, top executives of corporate organizations, other nonbusiness organizations, and outstanding pools of think-tank personnel. Really, two parties contribute to produce synergistic effects that are both supplementary and complementary each other.

In the next chapter, the management systems of Japan and the United States will be compared with the Korean management system. One of the basic reasons for including this chapter was that the unique features of the Korean management system will appear distinctive in comparison with the management systems of other countries. We chose the Japanese management system because of the similarity between the systems of the two countries. We also chose the American management system because it is and has been the typical management system of Western culture.

REFERENCES

Bae, I. K. The Heads of the Seven Largest Chaebol Groups (in Korean). The *Shin Dong-A* (April, 1985).
Kim, I. D. The Office of Planning and Control: The Think Tanks of Chaebol Groups (in Korean). *The Shin Dong-A* (February, 1988).
Likert, R. *New Patterns in Management.* New York: McGraw-Hill, 1961.
The Weekly Hankuk (September, 13, 1992).

10

The Korean Management System and Management Systems of Japan and the United States

Is the Korean management system unique and different from other management systems such as the Japanese and the American systems? The answer to this question is both "yes" and "no." All management systems have a common feature: They strive to enhance the performance of organizations in the most effective way to achieve the organizations' goals. The Korean management system shares with other management systems in this regard. From this perspective, we may state that all management systems function under universally applicable principles of planning, organization, control, leadership, and motivation.

However, the Korean management system is unique in that it is also culturally bounded. It strives to enhance the performance of organizations in the most effective way within the context of the Korean culture. Likewise, both Japanese and American management systems are unique because they function in the context of their own cultures.

A study of the Korean management system along with both Japanese and American management systems will highlight the unique features of the Korean management system. We have chosen the management systems of Japan and the United States just because these two management systems have had a significant impact on that of Korea.

When the Japanese occupied Korea from 1910 until the end of World War II, the Japanese brought a modernized or Westernized management system to Korea. The current Japanese management system is really a blend of their traditional management system with elements of the Westernized management system. While this management system was being practiced by the Japanese in Korea, Koreans integrated the Japanese management system into their own. Even today, the organizational hierarchical structure, for example, is mostly the same in both South Korea and Japan. All the hierarchical ranks of an organization are expressed by the same Chinese characters, although each country pronounces them differently. It is interesting to see the similarity between South Korea and Japan on official ranks in an organization:

Ranks	Japan	South Korea
Chairman	kaicho	hwoichang
President	Shacho	sachang
Executive Director	senmu	jeonmu
Managing Director	jomu	sangmu
Director	riji	eesah
Department Manager	bucho	puchang
Deputy Department Manager	jicho	chachang
Section Chief	kacho	kwachang
Deputy Section Chief	dairi	daerhee
Chief Clerk	kakaricho	kaychang
Regular Staff Members	Shain	sawon

Regardless of this similarity, the Korean management system has its own unique features because of the influence of the Korean cultural background. We will demonstrate these unique features when we investigate both the management systems of Japan and South Korea.

Since the end of World War II, the American management system has also had a great impact on the Korean management system. American culture has intruded into every aspect of South Korean society, and the Korean management system is no exception. More specifically, the American management system had been a symbol of effectiveness and efficiency in the past, and South Korean managers have tried to adopt many applicable concepts of the American system to their management system. Many Korean college professors have earned their masters and doctoral degrees from American universities and have taught their students what they learned from the United States. Koreans have adopted, for example, the term "marketing" because they cannot find an adequate word expressing the concept of marketing, although they have tried hard to locate a suitable Korean term.

Regardless of this massive infusion of American management concepts, the Korean management system still remains different from the American management system because of cultural influences on management practice. Although the Korean management system has never been analyzed as extensively as the American management system, distinctive features of the Korean management system have emerged from a comparative study with the American and the Japanese management systems.

Because the purpose of this chapter is to investigate the unique features of the Korean management system vis-à-vis Japanese and American management systems, a possible approach is to identify unique features of each management system and then to investigate their causes.

UNIQUE FEATURES OF MANAGEMENT SYSTEMS

In this section, we will investigate and summarize features of each of the three management systems and the causes of their uniqueness.

The Japanese Management System

Both American and Japanese management authorities seem to agree that the Japanese management system has the following characteristics:

- Consensus decision making
- Lifetime employment
- Group consciousness and team spirit
- Strong loyalty to employers and the organization
- Paternalistic leadership
- Personal approach
- Close cooperation between government and business
- Satisfactory relationship between labor and management
- Confucian work ethic
- Wa, or human harmony, as the motto
- Active participation of rank-and-file workers in quality circles
- Male-dominated management system

In the Japanese management system, a decision is not made until everyone involved agrees on the agenda. The decision-making process, therefore, is a consensus-reaching process, and individual decision making is out of the question. Decision making by the consensus process is called the "ringi" system (Yoshino 1971). A staff member in the lower hierarchy of the organization usually prepares a project plan, either through his own initiative or at the suggestion of his superior. The prepared plan is then circulated and reviewed throughout the organizational hierarchy. Each of these reviewers expresses his own reactions and views, and the original document is revised accordingly until a consensus is reached. After everyone involved agrees with the projected plan, the president finally affixes his seal of approval, making it a legitimate document.

Of course, this decision-making process is very slow, and not everyone involved may be satisfied with the decision because compromises are made to find common denominators. However, once a consensus is reached and the president agrees with the projected plan, everyone in the organization has an obligation to abide by such a decision and faithfully implement it for the sake of the organization.

Lifetime employment (Furstenburg 1974) is another characteristic of the Japanese management system. Once a recent graduate is employed by a company, he is guaranteed lifetime employment until he retires at 55 years old, although retirement at 60 has been an increasing trend.

As a result of this lifetime guarantee, some interesting concepts have developed in the Japanese management system:

- Seniority system
- Promotion
- Compensation
- Immobility

The seniority system or "nenko joretsu seido" is strictly applied, and the employee will reap the benefits of seniority if he stays with his company for many years. This seniority system is a major trend in the Japanese management system, even though some organizations have shown interest in the merit system of the United States. As a rule, promotion is based on seniority, and it is very rare that a subordinate competes with his superior for a higher position. Compensation is based on the seniority system, not on the merit system. Thus, the longer one stays with a company, the more one earns. Since an employee stays at a company for his lifetime, there is virtually no intercompany mobility for managers at various levels in the Japanese management system. Vacancies are usually filled from within the organization. Since employment is a lifetime commitment, recruiting bright and promising applicants is a critically important process for Japanese organizations.

In the Japanese management system, team spirit or group consciousness is more important than individualism. The term "individualism" is a contemptuous one in Japanese society. Individual aspirations must be subjugated to team efforts in order to maintain group spirit. The quality circle is a good example of team efforts used in the Japanese management system to enhance employees' productivity and satisfaction, and wa, or harmony among employees and even employers, is a catch phrase which functions as a catalyst to bind employees into a group and develop group spirit in an organization. Compromise among employees, not through confrontation, promotes wa.

Employee loyalty is also very strong in the Japanese management system. In fact, an employee is expected to show total loyalty to his superiors and the organization. In Japanese society, complete loyalty to superiors and the country is the highest virtue to be observed. Employers, in return, never fail to look after their employees' needs. Companies provide liberal fringe benefits programs, and the Japanese management system has to be understood in this context.

The leadership style in the Japanese management system (Drucker 1974) is based upon a very strict paternalistic and authoritarian pattern. Both employers and employees believe that a company is an extension of the family. The relationship between a superior and his subordinate is that of father to son, or oyabun-kobun. Thus, a superior treats his subordinates as he would treat his sons; he, in turn, is treated as a father figure by his subordinates (Kraar 1975). The well-structured management system with strict paternalistic leadership emphasizes a personal approach to motivate employees. Employees are encouraged to participate actively in all company affairs, are free to talk to their superiors, and their organization tries to operate an open atmosphere.

The relationship between government and business in Japan is exceptionally cooperative (Kaplan 1972). It does not necessarily mean that government controls business; rather, it means that business obtains strong support from the government for their endeavors. The government also protects business from outside competition through a protectionist policy, even though it has been curtailed significantly as a result of protests from the United States and other countries. The business community in Japan believes in the so-called guided policy of the government in which many talented and motivated government officials are able to advise business. This cooperation between the government and business has eventually led to "Japan, Inc."

One of the critical elements of maintaining a stabilized management system in Japan is a peaceful coexistence between labor and management. The Japanese have company unions, which are unable to lead a combative offensive. Both labor and management have to master the skill of compromise to avoid confrontation between them.

The Japanese live under the influence of the Confucian heritage in which hard, honest work and study are considered to be of the highest virtue. The Japanese understand clearly that they have to work hard simply because it is their custom, and hard work is an important social norm. It is the only way to guarantee their career success in the Japanese management system. They believe that their management goals can be achieved only through the use of wa (human harmony). Thus wa, a basic element of the Japanese management system, encourages a group spirit. Surprisingly, the Japanese do not officially mention profits as their prime emphasis.

Personal interaction is extremely important. Employers, therefore,

actively encourage employees to participate in and contribute to organizational activities. The quality circle is an example of a system through
which even rank-and-file workers are able to participate.

The Japanese management system is still a male dominated system,
although the number of female top executives has increased tremen-
dously in recent years. According to Takayama (1990), 23.1 percent of
nearly 800,000 Japanese companies surveyed have women presidents.
Traditionally, male-dominated Japanese society holds that a woman's
role is to maintain a fine family, raise children, and serve her husband.
The Japanese management system is now encountering a new environment in which women are becoming more aggressive in pursuing their
own rights and careers as professionals.

Overall, the Japanese management system has been very effective and
the envy of the rest of the world, although the system has experienced
some problems such as death from overwork, or karoshi (Plamann 1992).
Presently, however, the Japanese management system is changing from
a loyalty and stability-oriented system to an intrapreneurial and creativity-
oriented system in order to maintain a competitive edge.

The Korean Management System

Japan and Korea have much in common. Both countries have been
under the influence of the Chinese culture, and Chinese philosophy has
become the basis of their perception of the world. One Japanese news
reporter, for example, was so amazed at the similarity of the two cultures
that he said of Korea, "I felt like I had met a lost relative, a kinship that
was exactly the same as Japanese" (Japanese Look at Korea 1991). Part
of that kinship came from recognizing that art objects and Buddhism,
which he thought were originally Japanese or Chinese, actually came
from Korea. He was not alone in his amazement. More Japanese were
learning about Korea, partly because of the common history of their
nations and partly because of increasing trade with the region.

As was mentioned before, the Japanese management system had been
practiced in Korea for almost 40 years while Korea was under Japanese
colonialism. Logically, many ingredients of the Japanese management
system have been transmitted to that of Korea. Nevertheless, the Korean
management system is similar in many aspects to the Japanese management system and differs in others. The characteristics of the Korean
management system are as follows:

- Decision making by consensus with some qualifications
- Lifetime employment with some qualifications
- Individualism in group settings
- Loyalty

- Interorganizational mobility
- Significance of promotion
- Paternalistic leadership with qualifications
- Close relationship between government and business with qualifications
- Confucian work ethic
- Inhwa dangyul, or harmony and solidarity

Decision making by consensus is practiced in Korea as in Japan. The Koreans call it "the pumui system." Originally, the system came from Japan where it was used as the decision-making process by government officials. The process is basically the same as the ringi system, which was discussed in the section on the Japanese management system. However, there are some exceptions to it. For the most part, South Korean entrepreneurial founders made some bold decisions with or without consulting their top aids and announced them to their employees. The decision making by consensus process then is nothing but a formal process to rationalize and formalize the decisions made by the top executives.

Lifetime employment is also a traditional concept in the Korean management system. Once an employee is hired by an organization, he is guaranteed lifetime employment until he retires. An employer is very reluctant to lay off his subordinates even in times of recession. Contrary to the Japanese management system in which employees are rarely laid off, Korean employers lay off their employees in times of extreme hardship, as we discussed previously. Korean employees also accept layoffs as matters of fact.

Individualism in a group setting is a unique feature of the Korean management system. A professor in South Korea was amazed by the many groups that Koreans organized (Park 1991). Individual aspiration is as important as organizational goals for most Korean employees. In the Korean management system, group harmony or consciousness is strongly emphasized, and inhwa dangyul, group harmony, is one of the most popular mottos for many organizations. Nevertheless, it is not permitted to stifle individual aspirations in the context of group settings. One of the most important roles of superiors is, therefore, to promote individual aspirations in order to achieve organizational goals.

The concept of lifetime employment is limited in its application to the Korean management system because it is ignored by talented employees. Although an employee is guaranteed lifetime employment, employees are able to change jobs rather freely, if they are convinced that such a move will result in a more successful career. Interorganizational mobility is more common in South Korea than in Japan, where it has never been formally implemented.

Promotion is very important in the Korean management system because it becomes a crucial criterion which measures the success or failure of an employee. Since individualism in the context of group settings is as strongly persistent as is group consciousness, promotion may often be interpreted as a matter of life and death. Once an employee recognizes that there is almost no hope of promotion for him in the organization, he begins to look to other organizations in which he sees opportunities for promotion and growth. Since an employee's promotion is directly linked to family prestige and pride, the issue of promotion can be a fatal one for an employee.

The leadership style in the Korean management system in general is authoritarian and paternalistic. An organization is interpreted as an extension of a family, and relationships within the organization are similar to those within a family. However, there is no father-son type of relationship between a superior and his subordinates in South Korea as there still is in Japan. A manager is a superior, but he does not play a father role to his subordinates, and a subordinate in turn rejects any consideration of himself playing the role of a son to his superiors.

Some top executives of large *chaebol* group corporations manage their organizations through delegation of authority and the decentralized decision-making process. By and large, however, the Korean management system practices the autocratic and paternalistic leadership style.

The relationship between government and business is very close and cooperative. Traditionally, the government sets up industrial policy mainly through five-year economic plans, and business enterprises conduct their businesses by fulfilling these government plans. Business leaders sometimes take initiatives in proposing new ventures to be included in the forthcoming economic plan. However, it should be mentioned that businessmen have to have connections with the right government officials and political leaders for their businesses. Association with the wrong officials will eventually cause a devastating impact on their businesses.

The Confucian work ethic, or hard work, has been an important norm in organizations in South Korea. This work discipline was proved eloquently in the 1970s when many Korean employees were working in Saudi Arabia and other Middle East countries. People there were amazed and impressed by the discipline and long working hours of the South Koreans. Although this trend still continues, many employees today prefer to have leisure time instead of working overtime, a sure sign of a relatively affluent society.

Group spirit is as important in the Korean management system as in the Japanese management system. Both countries emphasize the importance of harmony among members in organizations by using one Chinese character to represent harmony. Koreans pronounce it hwa, while the

Japanese pronounce it wa. In the Korean management system, the emphasis is on solidarity and harmony in order to stimulate a group spirit.

However, there is a significant difference between the two group spirits. In Japan, group spirit is itself an ultimate goal because the Japanese function through groups. By contrast, to the Koreans, group spirit is a means to achieve their individualistic aspirations. They have learned an important lesson from their long history: Their individual aspirations are too critically important to be sacrificed, and they can be attained by promoting group spirit. This concept seems to be conflicting, and the Koreans are still learning to live in this world of conflicts. However, the Koreans have also learned the precious virtue of sacrificing their individual selves for the sake of their groups and their country. To understand the Korean management system, you must comprehend this complicated phenomenon of their behavioral patterns.

The American Management System

Many American management scholars and practitioners have generally agreed that the American management system has its own unique characteristics in the following aspects:

- Rationality and other American norms
- Individualism
- Impersonality
- Money-oriented
- Mobility and orientation toward short-range goals
- De-emphasis of the seniority system
- Protestant work ethic
- Profits as motivation

The American management system is based on rationality, which emphasizes efficiency. It is also based on other American norms such as openness, frankness, fairness, courtesy, and civility. While Americans are more interested in calculated objectivity, Oriental people are interested in emotional subjectivity. Americans are more open-minded, frank, fair, and courteous to others, and some Koreans actually lament this lack of civility among themselves.

The American management system is also based on individualism. Even though a conflict between individual goals and organizational goals and loyalty has been increasing in intensity, individualism is still dominant in the American management system. For example, many American employees believe that they can contribute to their organizations by their individual accomplishments. To American employees, the aspiration to achieve their individual goals comes before their loyalty and commitment to their organizations, thereby making them not as strong as their Japanese and even Korean counterparts.

Impersonality is another characteristic of the American management system. American employees clearly understand the difference between official and nonofficial or personal. Although connections are a relevant ingredient for career success in the United States, an employee will succeed only if he or she is capable of performing effectively. If an employee is qualified, he or she will be employed without other considerations. It is very ironic that Max Weber's impersonal approach to the bureaucratic management system still prevails in the American management system. Max Weber developed the concept of bureaucracies in which specialization, rationality, professionalism, impersonality, autonomy, and stability are core concepts.

Even if we admit that money is not a prime motivator for both managers and workers, it is still one of the most important elements in the American management system. The prestige and social standing of an employee is likely to be measured by his or her income. Therefore, an employee who works for wages or salary would always like to earn more. Likewise, the prestige of corporate executives is measured by their astronomical compensation packages. The American management system has been successful in applying this extrinsic reward system to promote effective performance.

In the American management system, interorganizational mobility is encouraged. If a manager stays with an organization until retirement, he or she may not be evaluated as an effective and capable manager. In a career path, an employee is encouraged to exercise interorganizational upward mobility five to six times. In our university, for example, a new president has been inaugurated who has served four different colleges as department chairperson, dean of the college, and vice president for academic affairs. American managers are highly motivated because of this upward interorganizational mobility. This is one way that the American management system is working. However, this mobility strongly encourages American managers to concentrate on and demonstrate short-range achievements and accomplishments so that they may prove that they deserve upward interorganizational movement. Long-range goals of organizations are not attractive to these short-range oriented career managers because these goals may not be beneficial to their mobility. In one sense, we can say that the American management system is thriving at the expense of accomplishing long-range goals.

In the American management system, seniority does not seem to be as important as it is in Japan and South Korea for two reasons. One reason relates to the compensation of entry-level employees. Their compensation is decided by the market price or marketability, not by an organization's compensation procedure. An entry-level employee's compensation then equates to that of senior members, whose compensations in some cases have been increased by a few percentages each year for 10 or even 20 years after their compensation packages were determined.

Another reason that seniority is unimportant relates to the merit rating system in which the compensation of employees is based on their contributions to their organizations. If a new employee contributes significantly to his or her organization, the employee's intrinsic and extrinsic rewards will be consistent with this contribution. Seniority does not play an important role in this situation.

A corollary of this phenomenon is the evaluation system. Evaluation is an important process in the American management system because the contribution of an employee can be identified mainly through an evaluation process. American employees are constantly evaluating people in the same organization and, in turn, are being evaluated constantly by them.

In our case, we (the authors) annually evaluate our chairperson or dean, the Vice President for Academic Affairs, the president of the university, and sometimes their nontenured colleagues. We also evaluate our tenured colleagues, when required. In turn, we are evaluated each year by our chairperson or dean, by the Vice President for Academic Affairs, and sometimes by our colleagues. In addition, each semester our students evaluate us.

The work ethic of the American workers and managers is based on the Protestant work ethic in which hard work is considered as the highest virtue and consistent with the Judeo–Christian doctrines. Americans believe that their accomplishments are the results of hard work.

As the American economy has allowed the development of an affluent society, many American managers and workers are more interested in a leisure ethic rather than a work ethic. Based on our own observation while living in the United States for more than a quarter of a century, we still believe that Americans are very hard working people. As workers, Americans are by no means lazy. They cannot be lazy because the American management system keeps them busy.

Although we have discussed extensively the social responsibility of corporations in the United States, producing profit is the prime responsibility of corporation managers. Although this may not be applicable to nonprofit organizations, such as educational and health care organizations, it is still the responsibility of the organization managers to generate enough revenue to continue their services to their customers. In profit-oriented organizations, managers express explicitly the importance of producing profits, while their Japanese counterparts are reluctant to mention profits openly.

Table 10.1 summarizes the unique features of the three management systems.

Table 10.1
Unique Features of Management Systems

	Japan	South Korea	USA
Decision making	Consensus, "ringi" system	Consensus, "pumui" system with some modification	By individual or majority vote
Duration of employment	Lifetime employment	Lifetime employment	No guaranteed employment
Individualism vs. group spirit	Team spirit extremely important	Individualism as strong as team spirit	Individualism persistent
Loyalty or commitment	Extremely strong	Very important	Not critically important
Seniority	Extremely important	Very strong	Strong
Mobility	Immobility	Flexible mobility	Free mobility
Management development	Exclusively inside promotion	Mostly inside promotion	Both inside and outside promotion
Formal evaluation	Not critically important	Not critically important	Crucial
Leadership style	Authoritarian/ paternalistic	Authoritarian/ paternalistic	Mostly participative
Compensation	Based on seniority	Based on seniority	Mostly based on merit rating
Government and business	Close relation and coopera-tion	Close relation and coopera-tion, but government dictates business often	No direct relation
Work ethic	Confucian work ethic	Confucian work ethic	Protestant work ethic
Mottos of organization	Wa, or human harmony	Inhwa dangyul, or human harmony and solidarity	Profit

CAUSES OF MANAGEMENT FEATURES

Understanding Management Systems

No two management systems are exactly alike. Although each system tries to attain high performance through effectiveness, each management system is unique in doing so. Each nation has maintained its unique cultural heritage, and these cultural differences have created unique management systems in each of the three countries. Any management system, therefore, can be expressed as a function of cultural identity.

$$\text{Management system} = f \text{ (Cultural identity)}$$

Cultural identity signifies a unique cultural heritage of people within a nation or a region. This unique cultural heritage can be identified by several variables such as language, religion, territorial location, social and political system, cuisine, clothing, and shelter. It seems that religion, territorial separation, and the political system contribute to forming value systems and are also relevant to cultural identity vis-à-vis the management system.

Every management system is regulated by the values developed and identified by the religions of the people. Religions, therefore, have important implications for the understanding of management systems of different nations.

People develop value systems more through religious doctrines because they teach us to distinguish between right and wrong. These doctrines also teach us to distinguish what is important from what is marginal. Both the Japanese and the Koreans have developed their respective value systems through Buddhism, Confucianism, and other Chinese religious teachings such as Taoism. Shintoism has influenced only the Japanese. Through Buddhism, people have learned their proper roles in this world in terms of Buddha, the absolute, and through Confucianism, people have learned the proper norms of behavior in society. Unlike other religions, Confucianism does not depict Heaven or other post-mortem reward; instead, it emphasizes maintaining and developing a moral society in this world. The Japanese and Korean value systems, therefore, are organized by the teachings of various religions. However, Shintoism is exclusively a Japanese concept.

The behavior of many Americans, by contrast, has been influenced greatly by Christianity. The religion has taught many Americans about God, the supernatural being, and the proper behavior in this world in the context of man's relationship to God. For many Americans, Christianity has been the only source of values because they seem to believe that it is the only legitimate and orthodox religion in the world. As a result, these Americans ignore other religions throughout the world, believing that there should be no other religion except Christianity. The American value system based on this acknowledgment can become a self-centered system. Eventually, this ethnocentrism may lead to a superiority complex about their own cultures and people as opposed to those of other countries.

Territorial location also has an impact on the management system because people develop behavioral patterns based on their environmental conditions. Although two nations share religious values, the people of each nation will develop different behavioral patterns based on where they live. Korea, for example, is a peninsula surrounded by the big powers of China, Russia, and Japan, who have interests in the Korean peninsula. This constant direct or indirect threat of intervention has had a profound impact on the behavioral patterns of the Koreans. Japan, on the other hand, as an isolated island country, has been able to maintain a stable society without experiencing major foreign invasions.

Although the Americans and English share basic values, they have developed different behavioral patterns because they reside in different geographical territories. Territorial separation partly explains the difference in behavioral patterns between the Japanese and the Koreans, despite their shared heritage of Buddhism and Confucianism. Therefore, the value system developed by the influence of religions has been modified by the impact of territorial separation. People of each nation preserve their unique value systems, and therefore have developed different management systems.

Cultural Identities of the Three Nations

As was discussed previously, each management system is formulated by the value systems that regulate the behavior of the people. Although other values are also important, the impact of religion and territorial separation are of outstanding importance. These different value systems, created by unique cultural heritages, have resulted in the unique cultural identity of each nation. Therefore, Japan, South Korea, and the United States have their own cultural identities.

One of the striking differences among these three nations is their conception of blood. While Korea is a blood-taboo society, both Japan and the United States are blood-prone societies. Koreans have developed a value system that prohibits bloodshed. Killing and being killed, except in extreme cases, became a taboo to Koreans. In the past, the lowest class, or the underclass, in Korean society was the class of butchers (Han 1989) who were engaged in killing and therefore dealt with blood. As a result, "son of a butcher" is a more profane term in Korean society than "son of a bitch." Foreigners were amazed that so few fatalities resulted from violent student riots and labor strife in South Korea. Because of their cultural heritage, students, workers, and the police are all aware that they should avoid bloodshed. A popular method of executing traitorous subjects used by kings in Korea in the past was to take poisonous drugs. This method is consistent with the Koreans' hatred of bloodshed. By contrast, the so-called harakiri, the practice of a type of suicide by using a sword, put Japanese lives at stake. While Japanese society encouraged the beauty of bloodshed, the Koreans totally shunned it.

These two different value systems vis-à-vis the blood concept resulted in a different understanding of the Confucian social class system in Japan and Korea. The social hierarchy or the social class system of the two countries is expressed by four Chinese characters. While the Japanese call them si-no-ko-sho, the Koreans call them sa-nong-kong-sang.

It is quite interesting to note the difference between the most noble classes in both Japanese and Korean societies. The Japanese considered the warriors as the highest class, or si. The Koreans respected most highly the men of literature, or sa, and held the warrior class in contempt. Historically, the man in military uniform has never been respected, except in occasional situations. The lower classes, such as farmers, manufacturers, and merchants, all rank similarly in both countries.

Why did the Koreans develop a blood-taboo society? Although the answer to this question is not so simple, we will attribute this phenomenon to Korea's proximity to China, the only major power to influence Korea for many years. Korea had been under the military protection of China and paid tribute to China in return. Like Japan, which since World War II has been under the military protection of the United States, Korea had no need to develop a strong military force except as a means of self-defense.

The political system is another factor in promoting cultural differences. The Koreans developed a centralized government structure in which the king was directly responsible for administration. A Korean needed swords only to protect the king when a group of rebels threatened the kingdom and a strong security or police force, rather than a strong military force. On the other hand, the Japanese had a system called feudalism in which feudal lords maintained their territories by fighting with other lords. The swords then became necessary.

The Americans have developed a blood-prone society. While they were moving westward, they carried guns in order to protect their frontiers from potential enemies. Even today many Americans keep guns, while Koreans are forbidden by law to possess them except as hunting rifles. Western culture, which the Americans inherited, respects the military class who fought in the name of God, king or queen, feudal lord, and country. In the United States, the military system is respected, even under a civilian government. Although the Reserve Officers' Training

Corps (ROTC) program exists in South Korea, Koreans are amazed by the many military colleges available in the United States. Aller (1992) stated, "Until Vietnam, all boys dreamed of being warriors."

Behavioral patterns of the blood-taboo society and the blood-prone society are different. If anyone knows that he is not in danger of being killed, then he can express himself in extreme manners without the fear of being killed. The Koreans have demonstrated an ultrabehavioral pattern and they have been told that they are very emotional and straightforward. It is not unusual that disarrays, protests, and quarrels are found occasionally in the Korean communities. The behavioral patterns of both the Japanese and the Americans are, on the contrary, quite different from that of the Koreans. Usually, they show orderly behavior and self-restraint. If they do not, they know that they may be killed.

The blood concept can also be linked to the family system of these countries. The Korean family system is unique in that the blood relationship in the family is extremely important. Traditionally, the Korean family does not accept the concept of adopted sons. Having his own son(s) is a Korean's supreme responsibility to his living parents and to his ancestors. The Japanese have developed a more permissive family system because the concept of adopted sons has been accepted throughout their history (Hirschmeier and Tui 1981). The Americans have demonstrated a most generous attitude toward adopted children. In a professional meeting, a participant told me (one of the authors) that he had adopted ten Korean orphans, although he had his own children. Americans raise adopted children as if they were their own, which is beyond the comprehension of many Koreans. We have been impressed with the beautiful adoption system in the United States.

The family system in Korea is crucially important because the Koreans perceive their society purely in terms of family. Their families were the only means of protection when the country had been invaded by foreign countries, and they showed little confidence in the government in case of an emergency. While the family system in both Japan and the United States is the basic foundation of their societies, they have never developed such an inviolable concept toward their family systems.

Behavioral patterns from this blood relationship show differences among these three nations. To the Koreans, filial piety is the mostly respected value. The Koreans accept totally the following advice from the New Testament, except for the term "in the Lord": "Children, obey your parents in the Lord, for this is right. Honor your father and mother (this is the first commandment with a promise) that it may be well with you and that you may live long on the earth" (Ephesians 5: 1–3). The Japanese, on the other hand, consider loyalty to their superiors as the most important value, although they also honor their parents. Neither filial piety nor loyalty to superiors are critically important to Americans.

Territorial separation or location has significant meaning in identifying unique behavioral patterns of the three nations. The territorial location of Korea deserves special attention. Korea is adjoined by China and surrounded by Japan. This strategic location resulted in constant invasions from China, Mongolia, and Japan, and it was impossible for the Koreans to counterattack these mighty neighbors. Survival as a nation has been constantly at stake, and Korea's utmost concern has been to preserve its independence. In other words, Koreans have lived for many years in an extremely insecure and adverse environment.

This has not been the case for Japan, an insular country. Traditionally, Japan has been safe from foreign invasions. The only exception was the invasion by Mongolia in 1281, but kamikaze, or the so-called divine wind, chased the Mongolians away (Takagi and Fukuda 1971). As a result, the Japanese have rarely been exposed to such an extreme situation. The Americans have never developed a sense of insecurity from outside invasions. Hence, the United States has been considered the most secure country on earth.

The sense of security or insecurity vis-à-vis territorial separation has promoted different behavioral patterns among these three nations. Because of their extreme sense of insecurity, the Koreans have developed a behavioral pattern of regulated individualism and ultrabehavior. For a Korean, no one except himself and his family is responsible for his safety and the survival of his family members. He must protect himself and his family by his own effort because the government never provides such protection. For their survival as a nation, the Koreans have to be persistent because they understand that negotiations and compromises lead to the collapse of the country. Therefore, an ultrabehavioral pattern is needed to survive. It is not accidental that South Korea had been an ultra anti-Communist country, and that North Korea remains an extremely rigid Communist nation even after the collapse of communism. Going to extremes has long been a survival strategy for Korea.

Since both the Japanese and the Americans have seldom experienced national insecurity and crises, their behavioral patterns are more moderate and prudent, and they have developed tolerance levels from different viewpoints. The Americans, in particular, encourage and respect different opinions.

Some nations have developed a mythology, while others have hardly dwelled on it. It seems that people with a mythical tradition are imaginative and have a tendency to apply their imagination to challenging situations of the real world. In other words, they seem to be more creative and innovative. People with little mythology, on the other hand, may have developed a dry society where few imaginations and innovations were developed.

There is a distinctive difference among these three nations in this

Table 10.2
Cultural Identities of Three Nations

Cultural identity	Japan	South Korea	USA
Conception on blood	Blood-prone society	Blood-taboo society	Blood-prone society
Blood relationship of family	Critically important	Absolutely important	Not critically important
Conception on mythology	Mythic nation	Nonmythic nation	Mythic nation
Conception on national security vis-à-vis territorial location	Sense of security	Sense of extreme insecurity	Sense of extreme security
Conception on FARRS: Family	Filial piety very important	Filial piety absolutely important	Filial piety not critically important
Alumni and education	Education is absolutely important and schools attended are critically important	Both education and schools attended are extremely important	Education is critically important, but schools attended are not critically important
Regionalism	Important	Critically important	Not critically important
Reciprocal consideration on well-being between superiors and subordinates	Absolutely important Loyalty to superiors is extremely strong	Very important Loyalty to superiors is strong	Not important Loyalty to superiors is not strong
State or country	National interest is prime concern	National interest is prime concern	National interest is not prime concern
Own perception	The Japanese are superior	No superiority complex	The Americans are superior, particularly among WASPs
Time/space	Present-oriented Less physical contact Sphere of space is narrow	Present-oriented Less physical contact Sphere of space is narrow	Future-oriented Frequent physical contact Sphere of space is broad
Perception toward the world	Nationalistic	Nationalistic	Cosmopolitan

regard. Both Japan and the United States were blessed with rich mythical backgrounds. The Japanese attributed the emperor system to the myth of "amaterasu o mi kami" or divinely originated kingdom, and have developed Shintoism to sublimate the myth into a religion. This myth still appeals to the minds of the most contemporary Japanese, and it has a significant impact upon their behavior. The Americans have inherited their mythology from the Greeks and Christians, and they have preserved this mythology with a great pride. Contemporary Americans are still being affected by these myths in their everyday behavior, for example, by their observance of Halloween.

The Koreans have also preserved some myths, such as the "tangun" myth. Tangun, the founding father of Korea, was said to be born in a bear. However, Korean myths have never appealed to the minds of the Koreans, and they rarely entertained them. They seem to remain merely as extinct volcano-type myths. In other words, the Koreans have lived in a myth-scant society, their myths having never had any impact on the behavior of the Koreans. This trend might have been inherited from Confucianism, which contains little mythology. The Koreans have never developed a Shinto-like religion with myths, nor have tales of Buddhism appealed to them to a great extent.

Although imagination, creativity, and innovation may be linked to the tradition of myths, it may be hasty to conclude that the Koreans are less imaginative, creative, and innovative than the Japanese and the Americans. It is also an inconclusive assumption that the Japanese are as creative and innovative as the Americans.

FARRS is a composite cultural identity because it includes much of the cultural heritage of a nation. FARRS is the acronym for family, alumni, regionalism, reciprocity, and state. Family means the family system and its relative importance in a society. Alumni signifies the attitude toward education in general and the relative importance of schools attended. Regionalism demonstrates the relative importance of geographical sectionalism in a society. Reciprocity means informal and moral obligation of superiors to the well-being of their subordinates and the reciprocal response of loyalty to them by their subordinates. State signifies the importance of the government to the management system in South Korea.

The concept of family is very important to the three nations because it is one of the founding pillars for each society. However, the nuance of the importance is somewhat different among these nations. To Koreans, the family system is everything, and filial piety has the highest priority in society. The effort of the Koreans to maintain blood-related purity in their families must be understood in this context.

The family system is very important in Japan as in other societies, but filial piety has never been their highest virtue. Japanese instead rank loyalty to their superiors higher than filial piety. The Americans share with the Koreans a belief in the importance of the family system. They respect their parents and obey their advice, but filial piety is not a high priority.

Education is important in the three countries. It is understood as a driving force toward economic growth and a high standard of living. Confucianism emphasizes the importance of education and learning, and the learned are respected in both Japan and Korea. Learning is a critical factor in South Korea because it is the only way to achieve a successful career for many Koreans, which used to mean becoming government civil servants. Today, an applicant still must pass the civil service examination to secure a government job, and must study hard to pass the test. Education thus has been a guarantee for a successful life. This tradition of the high priority of education currently prevails in South Korea.

The Japanese have developed a similar attitude toward education. Although samurai, or the warrior class, was the top class, they were strongly encouraged to learn. They were really warriors plus men of literature. Even before the Meiji Restoration, there were many terakoya, or schools, which taught basic learning skills to young children. Almost 800 of them existed in the Edo area in 1722 (Takagi and Fukuda 1971).

The Americans were no exception to this encouragement of learning. Their settlement of the new continent started with churches and schools, and education spread throughout the nation. Without the help of education, the Americans could not have accomplished such impressive achievements. Even today, the United States maintains one of the best postsecondary education systems in the world.

In these three countries, the schools attended have a profound implication on a person's life after graduation. Graduation from a prestigious university guarantees job security and assures a successful career. A Japanese must graduate from Tokyo University and a few other prestigious universities to achieve a successful career. A South Korean must graduate from Seoul National University or other top ranking universities.

In the United States, graduation from one of the Ivy League schools or other outstanding institutions will provide an American with a tremendous advantage over others. However, this trend is not so widespread in the United States as it is in Japan and South Korea. Even though the influence of the Eastern Establishment is powerful, graduates from other schools are given similar opportunities. In many cases, it is even more advantageous for students to graduate from local schools to develop their professional careers like lawyers, doctors, or politicians in their own state.

In Japan and South Korea, this restrictiveness has been alleviated these days to some extent. Yet a Japanese or a South Korean must graduate from one of the top-ranking institutions to assure a bright future.

We recently met a Korean-American professor of economics who told us that he was overwhelmed by the extensive dominance of the graduates of Seoul National University in every field in South Korea, such as government, business, and the legal system.

Regionalism or geographical sectionalism is a cultural heritage to these three nations. Each region of a country has developed unique perceptions, subcultures, dialects, and characteristics. In Korea, it is true that regionalism has developed generally along the borderline of state or doh. As the two former presidents and President Rho Tae Woo of South Korea are from the same region of "kyungsang doh," it is an accepted fact that they recruited many of their lieutenants and staff members from their own region. A Korean from this region would have a better opportunity to be chosen than would an equally qualified candidate from another region.

This trend is also strong in the United States where many unique characteristics of regionalism have developed. We (the authors) have been residents in the deep South for almost 20 years, and we have experienced the Southern sentimentality and hospitality from our American friends. American politics also show a strong tendency towards this regionalism. However, most Americans are treated equally regardless of their regional origins, except in politics where preferential treatment is given to residents of the state. As in Korea, regionalism in Japan becomes either a means to achieve ample opportunity or a great stumbling block. Japan has a much stronger tendency of regionalism than does the United States, but less than that of South Korea.

Reciprocity deals with the binding relationship between superiors and their subordinates in organizations both in Japan and South Korea. It is not a formal or legal relationship between them, but an informal and morally binding one. In Japan, this relationship is expressed in terms of "on" which means grace, mercy, or well-being implemented by superiors to their subordinates, and "ho-on," a reciprocal response, or informal requital of such "on" by subordinates to their superiors. The Japanese seem to commit themselves totally to this informal reciprocal relationship.

The Koreans also have kept this kind of tradition graciously. It has been a moral obligation of superiors to take care of the well-being of their subordinates. Reciprocally, it has been a moral responsibility of subordinates to repay to their superiors for the grace bestowed upon them. The Koreans become very angry and uncomfortable if this gracious reciprocal relationship is ignored or broken, either intentionally or unintentionally. However, it is not quite certain whether the commitment of the Koreans to this relationship is as strong as it is in Japan. It seems that the Koreans have never developed a sense of total commitment to it because of their demand for individualistic aspiration in a group context.

The Americans, with their Western cultural tradition, have never developed this informal and morally binding reciprocal relationship. Instead, they have developed a formal, legally binding, contractual relationship. Each person is eager to maintain his or her independence, the key element for individualism, without commitment to such informal obligations.

Perception of the relationship between individual life and national interests is another part of the cultural heritage among the three nations. There seems to be a different understanding of this relationship in Japan, Korea, and the United States. Both the Japanese and the Koreans have a tendency to link their personal activities with national interests, and officially have a strong feeling toward the well-being of their countries. They have inherited this tradition from the teachings of Confucianism in which loyalty to the king and the nation is the highest virtue. The Japanese have demonstrated this loyalty throughout their history, loyalty being a sacred word to them. The Koreans also have preserved this invaluable virtue, sacrificing their lives and their families during invasions by foreign adversaries. This phenomenon seems to be at odds with the highest virtue of filial piety in Korea. It is not paradoxical, however, since many Koreans are always dedicated to both supreme virtues, even though they place filial piety slightly higher than loyalty.

The Americans love their country, too. A strong sense of patriotism has prevailed throughout the history of the nation. We were impressed with the patriotism of Americans since we came to the United States. Americans' loyalty to their country is as strong as their Oriental counterparts. However, they have never developed a concept in which all of their activities must link to the national interests. Rather, they have promoted their own personal interests. We were overwhelmed by the American preference for Japanese cars by Americans regardless of a strong "Buy American" push by celebrities, thus making them seem more cosmopolitan than nationalistic. Of course, they understand tacitly that their own interests will eventually be consistent with national interests.

People develop either a superiority or an inferiority complex toward others. The Japanese have developed a superiority complex toward others, even though they had developed quite an inferiority complex toward Westerners during the modernization period after the Meiji Restoration. This superiority complex became very strong once Japan became one of the economic super powers after World War II.

The Koreans, on the other hand, have never developed this superiority complex. On the contrary, when Korea was occupied by the Japanese for almost 40 years until the end of World War II, they developed a strong inferiority complex. They were devastated both physically and mentally by the destruction caused by the Korean Conflict in the early

1950s. The Koreans, now free from this inferiority complex, have developed a sense of strong pride after accomplishing an impressive economic growth since the 1960s. The Koreans also take a pride in being the most homogeneous people on earth.

The Americans have developed a strong superiority complex, particularly White Anglo-Saxon Protestants (WASPs). In the past, Americans developed this superiority complex on the basis of race. They have also developed a superiority complex because they occupy a vast geographical territory and the world's wealthiest country. In addition, they consider themselves a mighty military power and the most advanced democratic country. This strong superiority complex seems to have lessened somewhat with the strong economic challenge from Japan, a non-Western nation, and from other Asian countries, such as South Korea.

Both the Japanese and the Koreans are more contemporary world-oriented people because the present is critically important to them. An old Korean saying emphasizes the relevance and importance of the contemporary world:

> Even if I am dumped in horse dung,
> Still, the life in this world is good to me;
> A living dog is better than a dead dignitary;
> Even if I am hanged upside-down,
> Still, the life in this world is good to me;
> My teeth are more important than my children;
> Eating a small bird's legs today is better than
> Eating a big slice of beef next year. (Yun 1970, p. 180)

Ancestor worship also focuses on the blessings for the present generation by the spirit of their deceased ancestors. In Korea, there is no concept of the end of human history, which indicates that the future is not particularly relevant to them.

To the Japanese, the contemporary world is critically important. According to Hayashi (1985), the past and the future revolve around the present. Human history, therefore, is not a straight line from the beginning to the end; instead, it circulates around the present.

The Americans, by contrast, have developed a clear sense of history from the perspective of time: past, present, and future. Human history is a straight line with the Alpha (beginning) and Omega (end) as the New Testament indicates. Human beings are moving along the straight line of history, the future world being as important as the contemporary world.

Neither the Japanese nor the Koreans engage explicitly in physical contact with others. Physical contact in public with the other sex has been somewhat taboo in the two countries. When greeting each other, the persons involved always keep a safe distance. There seems to be no difference between the Japanese and the Koreans in this behavioral pattern. There is, however, one critical difference between Japan and Korea. The separation between the opposite sexes is more strictly observed in Korea than in Japan. The bath shared by the opposite sexes in Japan is beyond the imagination of the Koreans. The Americans, by contrast, engage extensively in physical contact with others. Hugging a member of the other sex is commonly practiced, and no physical distance exists when they greet each other.

The sphere of space for both the Japanese and the Koreans seems to be narrow. Far too congested subway trains in both Tokyo and Seoul give an uncomfortable and uneasy feeling to both the Japanese and the Koreans, but they tolerate these inconveniences. The sphere of space for the Americans seems to be broad in that many Americans simply cannot tolerate such a narrow sphere of space.

Both the Japanese and the Koreans share the given space with other people. One can find bath tubs in Japan and in South Korea, which are shared by strangers who tolerate the shared space. It is unthinkable to Americans to share their bath tubs with strangers, and they have never developed a concept of a common bath tub. The Americans seem to pursue an independent sphere of space. Observing strict privacy is a decisive element in their lives. I (one of the authors) noticed women workers cleaning a men's restroom while men were using the facility in both Tokyo and Seoul. However, this practice is unimaginable in the United States.

The Japanese seem to be lacking in world perception because they do not have a religion that embraces all of humankind. They have preserved a nationalistic religion of Shintoism with an emphasis on Japanese superiority. Although many Japanese believe in both Buddhism and Confucianism, which have more universal content than Shintoism, the Japanese seem to have failed to extend their world perception to all humankind. According to one report of the Central Intelligence Agency (CIA) of the United States (Japan 2000 1991), the Japanese were criticized as racial discriminators, and as lacking the sense of responsibility toward the rest of the world.

Americans seem to be both nationalistic and cosmopolitan. We have been overwhelmed by the flag-waving of Americans. However, they are also cosmopolitan in nature because the country has been composed of people from many nations worldwide. Americans also have a religion, Christianity, which embraces all humankind. Americans sense that it is their responsibility to maintain the world order on the basis of their moral and religious values. They fulfill this responsibility through trial and error, but they seem to be very sincere in their endeavor.

The Koreans are very nationalistic and proud of their nationalism.

However, they have never considered that the world revolves around Korea. On the contrary, the Koreans have developed a sense of desperation because they have been at the mercy of the big powers. The Koreans are very sensitive to the world trend, because it will affect them one way or another. They seem to be more receptive to the outside world than the Japanese, and one proof of this is the number of Christians in both countries. In fact, Christianity is a Western religion to which the Koreans are overwhelmingly receptive. In South Korea, one out of four is Christian. The world's largest church, with more than a half million members, is in Seoul, Korea. By contrast, less than 1 percent of the Japanese are Christians. This difference may show that the Koreans are more cosmopolitan than the Japanese. There is a proverb in Korea: "Benevolence to humankind," or "hongik ingan," illustrating that Koreans have endeavored to embrace humankind in their perception of the world.

IMPLICATIONS TO MANAGEMENT SYSTEMS

As was discussed previously, each of the three nations has developed a unique cultural identity or heritage. The unique identities of the three countries have certain implications to their respective management systems.

Although both Japan and Korea have shared a heritage of Chinese culture in terms of Buddhism, Confucianism, Chinese characters, and literature, these two countries have developed different cultural identities. As a result, each country has developed its own unique management system, which has many similarities with and differences from each other. Between Japan and the United States and between South Korea and the United States, there are similarities and differences in the management implications of cultural identity.

There are striking differences between Japan and the United States vis-à-vis loyalty to superiors and perception toward the group and individualism. In Japan, loyalty to superiors is extremely important, and the Japanese people perceive the world in terms of groups. By contrast, in the United States, individualism prevails, and a sense of loyalty to their superiors has no significant meaning to the Americans.

Between South Korea and the United States, there are also differences. Since blood relationship has an intense significance to the Koreans, filial piety and family-oriented business have a great significance. In the United States, although there have been many family-owned and operated businesses in the American business history, no such emphasis is placed on family-oriented businesses.

The degree of similarities and differences of the managerial implications of cultural identity is shown in Table 10.3. The management systems

Table 10.3
Management Implications of Cultural Identity

	Japan	South Korea	USA
Blood on behaviors	Prudent, restraint, and orderly behavior	Occasional disorder and disarray Polarized behavior can be detected This polarized behavior may induce regulated individualism and aggressiveness	Prudent, restraint, and orderly behavior
Mythic tradition	Flexibility, creativity, and innovation	Less flexibility, conceptually less creative, and innovative	Flexibility, creativity, and innovation
Territorial location	Sense of security and long-range goal-oriented	Sense of extreme insecurity, and short-range goal-oriented	Sense of extreme security, and long-term goal-oriented
Family and blood relationship	Family member involvement to business is important	Family member involvement to business is absolutely important	Family member involvement to business is not significant
Alumni and education relation	High zeal for education Confucian work ethic Graduation from prestigious schools is critically important for career success	Extremely high zeal for education Confucian work ethic Graduation from prestigious schools is critically important for career success	Relatively high zeal for education Graduation from prestigious schools will help career success
Regionalism	Regionalism is not a critical factor for career success	Regionalism is critically important for career success	Regionalism is not significant for career success
Reciprocity	Reciprocal consideration is absolutely important Absolute loyalty to superiors and paternalism	Reciprocal consideration is critically important Strong loyalty to superiors and paternalism	Reciprocal consideration is insignificant Neither loyalty nor paternalism Absolute individualism

Table 10.3 (continued)

State or country	Concern for national interests precedes profits in many cases	Concern for national interests precedes profits in many cases	Separation between profits and national interests
Own perception	Tendency of ethnocentrism	Ethnocentrism does not exist	Tendency of ethnocentrism
Time/space	Past and future revolves around present in management Reluctance of physical contact	Past and future revolves around present in management Reluctance of physical contact	Time is understood as lineation of past, present, and future Frequent physical contact (such as hugging)
Perception toward the world	Narrow span of world perception Nationalistic	Narrow span of world perception Nationalistic, also semicos- mopolitan (Vogel 1990)	Very broad span of world perception Nationalistic, also cosmopoli- tan

of Japan and the United States reveal the most striking differences; the South Korean management system shows some common characteristics with both Japan and the United States; and the Koreans share loyalty to superiors and group behavior with the Japanese, but they also share individualistic attitudes in management with the Americans. On the other hand, the Koreans develop their individualistic aspirations in the context of groups.

Since the world is heading toward an interdependent global economy, a cosmopolitan attitude is critical. In this regard, the Americans have a definite advantage with some qualifications because they are cosmopolitan in nature. However, they are also ethnocentric. The success of American managers will depend on how they affect a compromise between these two conflicting features in the global economy.

Japan is an economic super power in the global economy. However, it is uncertain whether the Japanese will be the leader in the global community politically as well as economically, because they have never developed a cosmopolitan world perception. Many Japanese still believe that the world revolves around them, rather than they around the world. It is imperative for success in the global economy for the Japanese managers to develop a world perception independent of Japan.

Koreans are very nationalistic, and their world perception is limited.

Table 10.4
Significance of Managerial Implications

	Japan	South Korea	USA
Absolutely important	Loyalty to superiors Group behavior, wa or human harmony Reciprocal consideration between superiors and subordinates	Blood relation Filial piety Family member involvement to family business	Individualism Privacy Independence Profit
Critically important	Schools one attended Linkage of business to national interests Education Government-business relationship	Schools one attended, hwa or human harmony Linkage of business to national interests Education Reciprocal consideration between superiors and subordinates Regionalism Government-business relationship	Education
Important	Regionalism	Individualism	Schools one attended
Insignificant	Individualism	Ethnocentrism	Loyalty, Linkage of business to national interests, Reciprocal consideration between superiors and subordinates

However, they have developed a semicosmopolitan perception for their survival in the very volatile environment of the Korean peninsula. Some scholars (Vogel 1990) agree that the Korean managers have the capacity to be flexible in the global economy. Table 10.4 illustrates the significance of managerial implications among three nations.

CONCLUSIONS

There are many ways for us to comprehend management systems, one of which is to identify various aspects of management systems and their causes because it is our understanding that cultural identity or heritage is the main cause of these aspects of the management system. Each nation has its own cultural identity, formed by its own historical experience.

We can see the unique features of the Korean management system by comparing the Korean management system to that of Japan, with a similar cultural background, and the United States, with a different cultural background. We can use this approach to identify the similarities and differences of the management systems of these three countries. Both the management systems of Japan and of the United States have been very effective, and recently, the effective South Korean management system has attracted much attention because of the impressive economic growth that it produced.

In this study, we have traced some possible reasons for the effective management system in South Korea by comparing it with the management systems of Japan and the United States. This study has also demonstrated that different management systems can achieve effectiveness by different approaches. We acknowledge, of course, that there are many management concepts that cannot be explained solely on the basis of the dimension of cultural identity. We believe, however, that this approach will help readers to understand the unique features of the Korean management system.

In the next chapter, we discuss the profile of employees in the Korean management system. How do these employees conduct their everyday lives as employees of their organizations? How do they perceive themselves and their employers? How do they perceive their work? Since employees are a critical element in the Korean management system, it is imperative to understand South Korean employees in order to comprehend it.

REFERENCES

Aller, F. Rhodes Scholar Alessandra Stanley Most Likely to Succeed. *The New York Times Magazine* (November 22, 1992).

Drucker, P. F. *Management.* New York: Harper & Row, 1974.

Furstenburg, F. *Why the Japanese Have Been so Successful.* New York: Hippocrene Books, 1974.

Han, Y. K. *Hankuk Tongsa* (History of Korea). Seoul: Ulyumunhwasa, 1989.

Hayashi, S. *Management and Culture.* (I. G. Kim, trans.). Seoul, Korea: The Korean Economic Daily, 1985.

Hirschmeier, J., and Yui, T. *The Development of Japanese Business.* 2d ed. London: George Allen & Unwin, 1981.

Japan 2000: A Report of CIA. *The Asahi Shinbun* (June 9, 1991).

Japanese Look at Korea—and See Themselves (special advertising section). *The Wall Street Journal* (September 23, 1991).

Kaplan, E. J. *Japan: The Government-business Relationship.* Washington, D.C.: U.S. Government Printing Office, 1972.

Kraar, L. The Japanese are Coming—with Their Own Style of Management. *Fortune* (March, 1975).

Park, E. M. The Koreans and Groups. *The Dong-A Daily News* (December 18, 1991).

Plamann, S. Japan's Secret Shame: Overwork is Killing Thousands Every Year. *National Enquirer* (June 23, 1992).

Takagi, T., and Fukuda, K. *History of Japan* (in Japanese). Tokyo: Yomiuri Shinbun, 1971.

Takayama, H. The Main Track at Last. *Newsweek* (January 22, 1990).

Vogel, E. F. Korea Will Not Become a Resemblance to Japan. *Sasang* (Winter, 1990).

Yoshino, M. Y. *Japan's Managerial System.* Cambridge, Mass: The MIT Press, 1971.

Yun, T. R. *The Koreans* (in Korean). Seoul, Korea: Hyunamsa, 1970.

11

The Korean Employees

If the system applies both its human resources and nonhuman resources in the most effective way, any management system can be effective. Human resource management, therefore, is an indicator of management effectiveness, which was covered extensively in the previous two chapters. In this chapter, we will discuss human resources in the Korean management system from a micro-aspect rather than macro-aspect in order to understand how individual Korean employees work and how they perceive themselves within the framework of their organizations.

EXAMPLES OF KOREAN WORKERS AND MANAGERS

The following is a career profile of R. M. Kim who was promoted to a director (eesah) of the Hyundai Motor Company (Lee 1987). Kim was promoted to the new position after serving seventeen and one-half years in the company. He began as a staff member in October 1969 and was promoted to section chief (kwachang). He then served four years as a deputy department manager (chachang), followed by three and one-half years as a department manager (puchang). He became a director after serving one year as an associate director. Following the general guidelines for promotion from a tenured position, as described in Chapter 7, he received his retirement payment of 30 million won ($40,000 at the exchange rate of $1 to 750 won) as a tenured employee and deposited it in a bank. Kim never signed any paper of resignation from Hyundai as a tenured employee, because his company simultaneously documented for him his resignation and successive re-employment as a director, a nontenured position. After this promotion, he is no longer protected by the Labor Protection Act, which applies to rank-and-file staff members up through department manager.

Kim arrives at his office at 7:30 a.m., 30 minutes earlier than his usual routine since he became a director. He drives a company car, and has his own office with a female secretary. Kim begins his working day by reviewing the status of the departments under his jurisdiction. Responsible for exporting Hyundai cars to overseas markets, his task for the year is to export 400,000 units. During a typical day, he makes about 50 transactions over the telephone and makes decisions about 30 to 50 business matters, while department managers under him await his signature. Kim is so busy that he sometimes complains that he has no time even to go to the bathroom. Yet, he rushes to the president's office whenever the president calls.

He leaves his office between 7:00 and 7:30 p.m. from Monday through Friday and 3:00 p.m. on Saturday; he often gets home much later. He travels extensively for his company and attends monthly meetings at a factory several hundred miles away. At least once a month, usually accompanying top executives, he travels abroad.

Kim earns 1.3 million won ($1,733 at the exchange rate of $1 to 750 won) as a monthly salary. His net take-home paycheck was between 800,000 to 900,000 won (approximately $1,200) as of 1987. He also received bimonthly bonuses, which, each year, totalled 400 to 500 percent of his monthly salary. When he was a department manager, his salary was 890,000 won ($1,187) with a net take-home paycheck of 550,000 won ($733).

Some of the changes associated with his promotion from department manager to director include a larger and more luxurious office as well as an exclusive secretary to serve him. His company provides a company car with a chauffeur and pays all car expenses. However, some companies like Hyundai encourage directors to drive themselves in a company car. His salary and discretionary budget have increased significantly. No longer a passive employee who depends upon the directions and decisions of superiors, he has the authority to make some final decisions for the company. He leads his subordinates and makes critical decisions, based on his judgment and criteria. As a director, he is obliged to meet and entertain many people, including customers, sometimes until late at night. A director may require 24-hours-a-day, 7-days-a-week attention to fulfill his responsibilities.

Unofficially, a director is called a "star," implying that he is like a general in the military. Accordingly, it is very hard to be promoted to a director from a department manager. Only 3 percent of the department managers in organizations in South Korea will be promoted to the rank of director (Lee 1987). An exception is Daewoo Group, where 5 percent of department managers will be promoted to directors. When a department manager fails to be promoted to a director, his employment is terminated, and he has to leave his organization in his forties or fifties.

Unless he is promoted to an upper-level position of a managing director (sangmu), he will be terminated by his company.

Upon his resignation, he is eligible to receive his retirement or resignation payment as a lump sum. At Hyundai, the retirement amount is calculated according to the following formula: the average of the last three months' compensation multiplied by twice the number of years of employment after he became a director. If he were promoted to a managing director, three times the number of years of employment is the formula used to calculate his retirement pension; four times, if he were promoted to the rank of an executive director (jeonmu); and then to a vice president (pusachang); and five times, if he were promoted to a president (sachang). However, this practice is not applied uniformly to all organizations in South Korea. Each organization has its own formula for the calculation of retirement pension.

S. B. Park is a manager of the sales department at K company of the H *chaebol* group (Seo 1987). He is in his mid-thirties. He leaves his home at exactly 7:00 a.m. and becomes a company man when he punches his card in the punch card machine. Around 7:40 a.m., he plans his day's work and prepares for the 8:00 a.m. meeting with his superiors and other senior managers under him to discuss the business of the day. At 8:30 a.m., he calls a department meeting and gives directions to achieve the goals set by his superiors. After the meeting, his subordinates, mostly sales people, leave the office and start to call their existing and potential customers. Next he reviews business reports and reads information on company products. At midday, he entertains one of the important customers at lunch.

In the afternoon, he answers the inquiries for his subordinates. Around 5:00 p.m., his subordinates return to the office from the market and from their customers. He does not leave his office until his direct superiors have gone. Therefore, he usually stays past 9 p.m., ending a 12- to 14-hour workday. On his way home, Park drops in at a bar to broaden his business contacts. He finally gets home late at night.

In a company, department manager is the highest tenured position, which is guaranteed by the labor law, and four possible paths for future advancement. One is to be promoted to a director after being recognized for remarkable achievement by his superiors, a very lucky case. Another path is to retire when he reaches 55 years old, according to the legal requirement. The third possibility is retirement by job classification. In this case, any employee, including a department manager, must retire from the company if he cannot be promoted to an upper position within ten years. If an employee, for example, becomes department manager at the age of 35, he must retire from the company at 45 unless he is promoted to a higher position. The last path is to resign during his tenure as department manager, either to change jobs or to open his own business.

Many department managers are proud of their accomplishments in their organizations when they are promoted to department manager. However, at the same time, they also experience a sense of frustration, feeling that they may have reached their peak and their future may be bleak. The exceptions to this scenario are a few department managers who are fortunate enough to be promoted to director.

C. J. Kim, a section chief (kwachang) of a trading company, has been assigned to the New York office and is scheduled to begin work there in a month (Lee 1985). He was notified of this transfer three months before. He wakes up at 5:00 a.m., practices English for one hour, and has a convenient breakfast of a fried egg and cup of milk. (In Korea, there is no basic difference between breakfast and dinner.) He then rushes to a foreign language institute and practices English for another hour before arriving at his office at 7:40 a.m.

He begins his regular duties after reviewing a book of daily English practice and listening to business English cassettes in his room. Even while he is working, he practices English by himself. He usually leaves his company an hour earlier than his colleagues, at 6:20 p.m. and heads to a university for a foreign language class paid for by the company. He returns home around 10:00 p.m. after studying almost two hours at the language institute. He still practices English for about two more hours before finally going to bed around midnight.

M. S. Kim, a deputy section chief (daerhee) of a trading company, was responsible for exporting textile goods (Kim 1985). He left his home around 6:30 a.m. after taking a sandwich and a cup of milk, which is not a typical breakfast in South Korea. While he was driving his small car, he planned his day's schedule and practiced French with the audio cassette in his car. It was useful to him to comprehend French because his assigned territory was Europe and Africa. He arrived at his company around 8:10 a.m., after studying French at a foreign language institute. He was preparing himself for another warlike day, and he was determined to fight and win.

During his office hours, he negotiated extensively with potential buyers and guided them through manufacturing plants for on-site inspection. In addition, he entertained his buyers with a sightseeing tour and dinner. Usually he arrived home around midnight to be greeted by his wife's complaints about his late arrival.

EMPLOYEE PERCEPTION

It is important to understand the perception of employees about their work, their superiors, the nation's economy, and labor unions. In this section, we will discuss worker perception about these areas on the basis of a survey conducted by the Economy and Technology Research Center of the National Federation of Businessmen. The sample surveyed 1,915 employees from 111 corporations who participated in the 1977 survey.

The first question the survey asked was, "What is the most important criterion when you select a job?" To this question, employees responded as follows:

Promise of future work	31.4%
Without serious considerations	21.1%
Developing individual capacity fully	16.3%
Worthwhile work	15.3%
Obtaining technical know-how	6.5%
One of the best companies	4.1%
Better compensation	2.5%
Friends, alumni in the organization	1.5%
Better working conditions	0.7%
Eight working hours a day	0.6%

Employees in South Korea are keenly interested in working for organizations where they can develop their potential. The promise of future work, developing individual capacity, and worthwhile work are very important criteria for their jobs. Surprisingly, compensation was not an important criterion to them.

To the question, "What is the most important reason for working?" Koreans employees responded as follows:

To have a better life	38.8%
To utilize my potential	28.9%
To earn livelihood	13.7%
Without serious considerations	5.9%
To support my family	4.6%
To be successful in society	4.8%
To contribute to my country	3.3%

Yearning for a better life is understandable because the Koreans lived in poverty for many centuries. Freedom from such poverty had been the national slogan or catchphrase when the first five-year economic plan was implemented in the early 1960s. Along with a better life, the Korean employees expressed their interests in fulfilling their potential in their organizations.

The third question was, "Will you work at your present company until you retire?" This question is an interesting one because it relates to the issues of employee loyalty and lifetime employment. The response was as follows:

I think so.	35.2%
I have no comments now.	33.6%
I want to transfer to a company that guarantees my future career.	13.4%
I consider changing jobs for better compensation.	12.1%
Others	3.1%
I work here because I have nowhere else to go.	2.6%

Only one-third of the respondents confirmed that they would remain with the company until they retire. A majority of them implied that they would leave their company if a better opportunity arose. Therefore, it remains an open question whether Korean employees have a strong loyalty to their organization. The response to this question also reflects that the Korean employees are not as interested in lifetime employment as their Japanese counterparts.

In the previous chapters, we emphasized the unique features of the Korean management system in the sense that Korean employees are very individualistic in group settings and quite mobile from one organization to another if a better opportunity is offered to them. The response to this question once again reaffirms our observation and study. In a round table talk, a company manager mentioned that there would be no employee in South Korea who never thought of changing his job (Kim 1984). This survey is also consistent with another survey conducted by the Korean Chamber of Commerce (1984). While employees expressed their willingness to change jobs whenever a better opportunity is offered (42.3%), only 18.4 percent of them responded that they would stay with their companies.

The fourth question was, "How do you perceive the nation's economy and the role of businessmen?" The following is the response from the Korean employees:

Businessmen play an important role in the growth of the economy.	34.7%
It was workers, not businessmen, who have contributed to the economic growth.	29.6%
Our government has led the economic growth, and corporations have grown with government support.	22.6%
I don't know.	13.1%

The Korean employees perceived that the government, businessmen, and workers have contributed equally to the growth of the national economy. It seems to be a very healthy perception. Really, the great accomplishment of the South Korea economy, one of the fastest growing economies in the world in the past three decades, is the outcome of the endless dedication of workers, managers, entrepreneurs, and the government.

The fifth question sought the workers' attitudes toward businessmen in general: "How do you evaluate businessmen?" The Korean employees responded as follows:

They have utilized their entrepreneurial talents.	26.0%
They are very industrious and hardworking.	18.0%
I don't know much about businessmen.	17.5%
They made a fortune through their self-interests and unethical activities.	15.7%
They have been successful through their intelligence and technical know-how.	12.6%
They made a fortune by mere luck.	10.2%

In general, the Korean employees agreed that businessmen made their fortune by hard work and the use of their entrepreneurial capacity. Although some employees criticized businessmen, it seems that they evaluated the Korean businessmen rather objectively.

The sixth question was more specific concerning their own organization. The question was, "How do you evaluate the owner-president of your company?" The following is the response from the employees:

I have no comments.	24.6%
I respect him greatly.	23.3%
He is a good businessman.	19.0%
He is a man who considers business interests and the well-being of the employees equally.	16.1%
He is too profit-oriented.	13.3%
He is a man of many faults as a businessman.	2.8%
He is an incapable person.	0.9%

It is rather surprising that almost one-fourth of the employees sampled responded that they had no real opinion concerning their owner-president. However, the majority of the respondents confirmed that their chief executive officer was a respected businessman.

The next question asked the employees about their perceptions of their own company. Their response to the question, "How do you evaluate your own company?" was as follows:

My company is a relatively good company.	29.9%
My company is a mediocre one.	22.9%
My company is a model of a good company.	21.1%
I have no comments.	14.4%
My company is not an attractive one.	9.6%
My company has many unethical elements.	2.1%

One-half of the respondents expressed their pride in the company where they worked. It is interesting to see contrasts in the Korean employees by their perceptions in their responses to Question 3 and this one. Ironically, in these two questions, the Korean employees expressed interests in leaving their company for better opportunities, although their company was a fine one.

The eighth question was one concerning future prospects of their company: "Do you believe that your company will grow in the future?" To this question, the Korean employees responded as follows:

The company will grow rapidly.	38.1%
The company will grow slowly.	33.1%
The company will maintain the status quo.	14.6%
I don't know.	8.7.%
The company will suffer a setback.	5.5%

Once again, the Korean employees expressed their optimism about the future of their company. It may be worth noting that the mid-1970s were prosperous years for the Korean economy mainly because of the investment boom of the Middle East countries and active participation of many Korean companies there. Workers and businessmen rushed to this region and earned oil dollars by working hard, long, and effectively. Everything seemed to be rosy.

The ninth question was, "The nation's economy has grown rapidly. Has your standard of living improved accordingly?" The Korean employees responded as follows:

It will improve in the future.	54.2%
My standard of living has not improved.	23.3%
I don't know.	12.5%
Yes, it has improved.	10.0%

It is surprising that only 10 percent of the Korean employees sampled responded affirmatively to the question. Then again, perhaps this response should be expected considering the South Korean government had a consistent policy of concentrating wealth among the few under the pretext of promoting rapid economic growth. In one sense, the South Korean economy had produced an "economic miracle" at the sacrifice of workers and lower level managers, but this has changed rapidly since the June uprising of 1987.

The tenth question was about labor unions: "Are labor unions necessary in South Korea?" To this question, the employees responded as follows:

Yes, we must have labor unions.	52.3%
It is better to have labor unions.	35.2%
I don't know.	7.7%
No, it is not necessary to have unions.	4.8%

The Korean employees decisively felt the need for labor unions to protect their interests. It is well known that the South Korean government had suppressed the union movement in the name of rapid economic growth. The government tried to convince the employees that South Korea needed to accumulate the national wealth first. It was not an important issue to the government how to divide the wealth among the people. Labor unions have grown rapidly in number and have exercised power and influence in the Korean society since the June uprising of 1987.

Korean employees' perception of work is very healthy. According to one report from the Korean Chamber of Commerce (1992), the most important thing to them is career (39.8 points), followed by family (30.8 points), leisure (16.1 points), community service (7.1 points), and religion (6.4 points). This finding contrasts with findings of other countries. Japan, for example, shows similar results by rating the career first (36 points) followed by the family (35 points). However, American employees put family first (34 points), followed by career (25 points). British employees show a trend similar to that of their American counterparts by putting family first (40 points), followed by career (22 points).

We have emphasized that the family system is most important in South Korea, but this survey shows otherwise: career precedes family. With a moment's reflection, however, we can understand that there is no inconsistency between our assertion that the family system is of prime importance and the result of the survey. The survey implies that it is an employee's career that produces family prestige and pride. Without career, no family prestige and pride can be achieved. In South Korea, these two elements, family and career, are therefore complementary to each other.

To the question, "Why do you work?" Korean employees responded: "because the work is assigned to me" (81.7%), and "to earn money" (24.6%). By contrast, monetary reward was the most probable reason why Japanese employees work (73%). It is not clear whether Korean employees are motivated more by intrinsic rewards than their Japanese counterparts.

Only 28.8 percent of Korean employees were satisfied with their life, and the majority of them were moderately satisfied (62.3%). A similar response was shown by the survey of Japanese employees: satisfied (24%), moderately satisfied (66%), and not satisfied (10%). By contrast, American employees were very satisfied with their life (80%).

This survey indicates that Korean employees are eager to work for career success, which brings prestige and pride to their families. In one sense, the miracle of the Korean economy is a reflection upon hard working employees.

EMPLOYEES' STRESS

Korean employees experience painful stress in their work environments. The stress is mainly related to three factors: (1) maintaining a satisfactory interpersonal relationship with their colleagues, superiors, and subordinates; (2) the fear of being laid off from the job; and (3) the stress of uncertainty of the future course of life.

Korean employees deal with these stresses by establishing coping strategies. One of the most important career successes for Korean employees is to maintain a satisfactory relationship with their colleagues. On one hand, employees are colleagues, and on the other, they are competitors or potential enemies. The best strategy for this stress is to mingle with their colleagues in small restaurants after work. They eat together, drink together, and chat together to resolve the stress of maintaining good relationships with each other. Usually they come home late, but Korean employees admit that this is a price they have to pay to overcome this stress.

Some companies have official mechanisms to help their employees cope with this stress. Sunkyong Group, for example, has an official mechanism called a "can meeting." This is a two-day meeting each quarter of a year, when employees freely discuss any subject. Other companies also apply similar mechanisms for the same purpose.

Stress is also caused by an employee's relationship with his or her superiors, and coped with either through confrontation, compromise, or obedience. Korean employees apply all three strategies to this relationship. When they confront their superiors, they must prepare to be penalized by a delay in promotion, demotion, or at worst, resignation from their organizations. This is a courageous but very risky strategy. Many Korean employees choose the safer strategies of compromise or obedience rather than a confrontation with their superiors, although confrontation between superiors and subordinates is not rare. Koreans, considering their behavioral characteristics, are not afraid to confront their superiors.

Superiors also develop stress trying to maintain satisfactory relationships with their subordinates. In Korea, a reciprocity relationship exists between a superior and his or her subordinates. A superior expects loyal dedication from subordinates, and he or she, in return, must take care of their well-being. The sales department of a men's clothing company, for example, suffered a severe sales decline vis-à-vis its competitors. Top executives punished the entire department by means of a salary cut. The department manager, as the superior of his subordinates, called the wife of each of his subordinates explaining the reason for the salary cut and expressed a sincere apology for the disgrace of her husband. He explained to each that it was not her husband's fault and that he, as the department manager, was responsible for the unfortunate result (Kwon 1985). He continued to call these wives until late at night. It must have been a stressful experience for him, but he tried to cope with his stress by honest confession and direct confrontation to the family members of his subordinates.

The chance of being laid off from one's job is a source of stress to most Korean employees. Layoffs take place when a company acquires another company, two companies merge, or a severe recession hits the economy as a whole. In these situations, companies often resort to employee layoffs across the board, affecting both white collar and blue collar workers. Samsung Electronic, for example, established a plan to reduce its nonessential work force of 13,000 by half by the end of 1994 (Song 1992). Many chaebol corporations and other companies also established plans to restructure their organizations into lean and mean organizations, which resulted in laying off employees, sometimes unmercifully. One employee found out that he was laid off from his company by finding that his desk and chair had been literally removed by the company, leaving him with no room to work.

There seems to be no remedy for coping with this stress. Many Korean employees try hard to cope with stress by locating another job, and some take extreme measures. For example, after learning that they were laid off from their organizations, some employees hid the fact from their families. Each morning, they pretended to go to their offices, and they came home late in the evening. Usually they spent their days in a park. Even though these are rare cases, it is not a healthy way to cope with the stress. In many cases, employees were successful in landing another job or starting their own business. During this painful experience, they still received warm understanding from their family members.

Preparing a future course of life is a source of grave stress to Korean employees. When he misses a promotion, an employee has to resign from his organization within a certain number of years as required by the organization. Promotion is, therefore, vital for his career success, but the path to promotion is extremely narrow and competitive, and severe stress accumulates accordingly. To cope with this stress, an employee who resigns must find another job. It seems to be relatively easy for an unemployed person in his thirties to locate another job, but it is by no means an easy task to find another job for an unemployed person in his forties. He may thus have to find the means to start his own business.

With some exceptions, an employee must retire from his organization when he reaches 55 years old, still a relatively active period in his life cycle. Unless he is satisfied with his retirement pension, a retiree has to find a second career. This is not an easy task, and causes severe stress. One way to cope with it is to accept retired life and adjust to a different lifestyle. Another way to cope with this stress is to actively seek a meaningful second career by opening up a business. A third way to cope is to go to the United States to begin a second life. Many retirees from South Korea emigrate to the United States and start their own business, such as a dry-cleaning business. Since they have the financial resources of a retirement pension and working experience, retirees find it relatively easy to start their own businesses. Of course, they also count on the social security and other benefits provided for senior citizens in America before they emigrate there.

FEMALE EMPLOYEES

Traditionally, the Korean society has been male-dominated. Although the government has strongly emphasized equal employment for women, discrimination against female employees still exists in the Korean management system. Four companies that advertised to recruit only males were fined two million won each ($2,564 when the exchange rate was $1 to 780 won). Women have been discriminated against in both compensation and promotion, and some organizations do not even provide any opportunity for promotion for women employees.

In Korean organizations, women have to demonstrate two characteristics: work capability and femininity. Unless a women demonstrates both characteristics, her days in the organization may be numbered. However, as a woman advances on the organizational ladder, her work effectiveness becomes more crucial than her femininity.

Women have been challenging this discrimination. The number of law suits against organizations has recently been increasing significantly, according to one seminar sponsored by the Korean Friendly Organization for Women. In the seminar, two women employed by a university disclosed that they had filed a suit against the university after learning that they earned only one-fifth the wages of their male counterparts (Discrimination Against Women Workers 1990).

In 1990, there were 3.5 million female workers, of which 30 percent were married, according to the Ministry of Labor (1991). In the government, there were 180,000 female civil servants, or 24 percent of the entire civil servants, and 15 of them were heads of their bureaus, a high position of the government hierarchy according to the Ministry of Government Administration (1991). These government administration statistics show that female employees are gaining power in the Korean management system.

A RECENT TREND

Time management is an important phenomenon in the Korean management system. Many employees in the Seoul area leave their apartment complex at around 6:40 a.m. without eating breakfast to avoid the deadly rush hour traffic. They take their breakfast at fast food restaurants and snack shops near their offices that thrive by meeting the needs of their customers. These employees then rush to their offices to start work.

Korean employees are very serious about maintaining good human relationships inside and outside of their organizations. One sure way to do this is to participate in special events such as weddings and funerals. According to a survey by Samsung Life Insurance (1992), a male employee spends a little over 29,000 won ($37.20 at the exchange rate of $1 to 780 won), and a female employee spends 18,000 won ($23.10), for each wedding or funeral of his or her colleagues and friends. On the average, it accounts for 6 percent of the monthly living expense for Korean employees and represents a relatively heavy burden for them.

Korean employees have been working long hours (more than 50 hours per week) for more than 30 years. However, this trend has been changing. According to the Korean Labor Research Center (1991), Korean employees worked 48.2 hours per week in 1990. Since the law was revised to specify 44 hours of work per week in 1989, working hours will continue to be reduced in the future.

The work habits of the Korean employees have also been changing. In the past, income was their top priority. Many worked long and hard in order to make more money at the expense of their leisure, health, and family. These employees were desperate to free themselves and their family members from the absolute poverty that had plagued the Koreans for so long.

Now Korean employees are in the process of changing the priorities in their lives because they earn relatively generous incomes. Many Korean employees prefer leisure with their family instead of working long and hard and avoid working overtime. It is therefore not unusual to find a manufacturing plant's recruiting notice that emphasizes no overtime.

South Korean employees are becoming like the Japanese employees who hate the three K's: kiken (dangerous), kitsui (difficult or demanding), and kitanai (dirty). In the South Korean manufacturing industry, for example, there were five help seekers (employers) for one employment applicant in the first quarter of 1990, because Korean manufacturing workers believe that factory work is a hard job with low wages (Bae 1990). In order to cope with this trend, employers have been actively seeking workers from other countries, an unthinkable occurrence even a few years ago. However, in 1992, the job market was tight even for manufacturing workers because of the sluggish economy, making it even more difficult for college graduates to secure employment in their areas of specialization.

No management system can be completed without including social responsibility and ethical issues of organizations. In the next chapter, we must examine the Korean management system in terms of its social responsibility and ethical issues.

REFERENCES

A Survey of Employment. Seoul: The Ministry of Labor, 1991.

Bae, I. J. Nobody Wants to Work at Factory. The Dong-A Daily News (June 21, 1990).

Discrimination Against Women Workers for Promotion and Compensation Still Exists. The Dong-A Daily News (November 10, 1990).

Female Government Officials. Seoul: The Ministry of Government Administration, 1991.

Kim, C. U. Ten Years After Joining a Company (in Korean). The Dong-A Daily News (January 17, 1984).

Kim, K. M. Don't Lose Your Buyers (in Korean). The Dong-A Daily News (April 2, 1985).

The Korean Chamber of Commerce. A Survey of Employee Attitude Toward Their Jobs. Seoul: The Korean Chamber of Commerce, 1984.

——. International Comparison of Employee Attitude Toward Work. Seoul: The Korean Chamber of Commerce, 1992.

Korean Labor Research Center. Labor Trend Analysis, 1991.

Kwon, S. J. Rewards and Punishment (in Korean). The Dong-A Daily News (May 3, 1985).

Lee, I. K. Foreign Language Practice: Talking English Even in Sleep (in Korean). The Dong-A Daily News (May 10, 1985).

Lee, S. H. Life of Directors, Stars of Chaebol Groups (in Korean). Monthly Chosen (June, 1987).

Samsung Life Insurance Company. A Survey of Monetary Gift by Korean Employees (in Korean), 1992.

Seo, Y. K. Life of Department Managers in Their Thirties (in Korean). The Weekly Kyunghyang (April, 1987).

Song, T. K. To Make Lean and Mean by Large Enterprises (in Korean). The Hankuk Daily News (September 11, 1992).

12

Social Responsibility and Ethical Issues

Both business and nonbusiness organizations have obligations to society to fulfill social responsibility and to conduct their businesses ethically.

SOCIAL RESPONSIBILITY

There are two different viewpoints concerning the social responsibility of organizations to society. Milton Freedman emphasizes that the social responsibility of business, for example, is to fulfill economic performance by maximizing profits (Freedman 1962). His principle can be applied to any nonbusiness organization as well as to schools, churches, and hospitals. All of these organizations have their basic functions to fulfill — educating students in school, ministering at churches, and treating patients in hospitals.

However, there is another school of thought that insists organizations must play an active social role in the society in which they function. Keith Davis and R. L. Blomstrom (1980) represent this school. They emphasized that business organizations in particular have social responsibilities to fulfill along with the responsibility for fulfilling their basic mission of producing maximum profits. In the United States, the social responsibility of organizations include providing support for:

1. Civil rights against discrimination
2. Ecology by protecting the environment
3. Consumerism
4. Protection of employees' well-being

Of course, some conflicts develop between the basic missions of organizations and their social responsibilities. Business organizations, for example, are unable to maximize profits if they fulfill all of these social responsibilities. Davis and Blomstrom (1980), however, stressed that fulfilling social responsibilities will eventually pay off by connecting directly to profits.

To Americans, these missions may seem to be mutually exclusive, but most Korean corporations realize that they can accomplish both — producing profits and fulfilling social responsibilities. In addition to being profitable, the corporations also recognize that it is imperative for them to meet their social responsibilities: promoting the well-being of their employees, protecting the environment, producing goods and services to satisfy their customers, and promoting equal opportunity for women. Corporate managers must establish a trade-off between profits and social responsibility, either through their own initiatives or by the enforcement of laws. Laissez-faire capitalism is gone forever from the management system of South Korea. Socially responsible capitalism is functioning instead, despite many problems. Even some *chaebol* corporations continue to pollute environments because it is less expensive to pay fines than to install costly environment-cleaning equipment (Paying Fines 1992). Sometimes government inspection teams accept bribes to keep silent — a problem that we will discuss in the next section.

However, the time has come for corporations to pay serious attention to social responsibility. Under the regime of President Rho Tae Woo, corporations recognized that they would have to promote the well-being of their employees. Otherwise, labor unrest might become violent. According to a survey of the Korea Employers' Federation of 673 corporations in 1989, a majority (70 out of 100 points) of employers responded that they increased employee benefits simply to prevent labor strife. Workers' demand for increased benefits was another important reason (52.4 points), followed by traditional practice (41.5 points), and the company's profit increase (36.1 points).

In the Korean management system, these two different viewpoints on social responsibility with some modifications have strong supporters. There are many businessmen who claim that the basic mission of business organizations is to produce profits. If they fail to do so, they are failures. Events in the shoe industry in South Korea illustrate this case. Massive bankruptcies of shoe manufacturing companies in Pusan in 1992 brought about many severe social problems. Employees lost their jobs, and some of the more depressed persons committed suicide (Kim 1992).

Although maximizing profits is a crucial mission for businesses in South Korea, most business persons (entrepreneurs and managers) are keenly aware of the importance of fulfilling social responsibilities in addition to making profits. In South Korea, there has never been racial civil rights issues as in the United States. The Koreans are one of the most homogeneous people in the world, and their society is a relatively equitable one for opportunities and career success.

An area of civil rights at issue in South Korea is discrimination against women. The Korean society has a tradition of discriminating against women extensively. In the past, church buildings were built in a unique fashion so that men and women could not see each other. Both junior and senior high schools are organized by sex into all male schools and all female schools. Even when coeducation does exist in these schools, students are separated by sex into all male and all female classrooms.

The role of a woman is strictly confined to her family as a wife, a mother, and a daughter-in-law. There have been strong barriers against women in career professions except in a few female-dominated professions such as nursing. However, this tradition has been changing recently. Most colleges in South Korea have implemented coeducation systems where female and male students sit side by side. There are many career women such as college professors, lawyers, medical doctors, and government officials, but in business organizations, women executives are almost nonexistent unless they start their own businesses as entrepreneurs.

There has been steady progress in breaking this long cherished tradition in South Korea. No organizations recruit male applicants only. In 1992, close to 200 corporations were warned by the Ministry of Labor to eliminate their discriminatory recruitment policies. In 1992 for the first time, Samsung Group recruited male and female job applicants indiscriminately. Female college graduates accounted for 13 percent of the total of 11,600 applicants for 2,650 job openings at Samsung. Although other major groups did not follow the practice of Samsung Group, equal opportunity employment for women is expected to improve steadily simply because the number of educated women has been increasing dramatically in recent years, and the traditional perception toward women has been changing slowly but significantly. According to the Ministry of Government Administration (Kim 1991), women accounted for 23.7 percent of the total government employees in 1989.

One of the unique social responsibilities of Korean organizations is based on the reciprocal principle, a kind of covenant relationship, between employers and employees. Employees must show their loyalty to their superiors; employers, in turn, are obliged to enhance the well-being of their subordinates. Many business corporations support their employees in many ways. Employees receive financial support for education from their organizations, and corporations provide scholarships for the education of employees' children. Daewoo Group, for example, awarded the scholarships listed in Table 12.1.

Corporations not only pay attention to the education of employees'

Table 12.1
Scholarships for Employees' Dependents

Year	Number of employees' children who received scholarship	Amount (in thousand won)	
1982	241	52,041	($65,000)
1983	347	78,359	($98,000)
1984	434	50,664*	($63,000)

Source: Song, I. S. (1984). *Social Services of Corporations* (in Korean). Seoul: The Korean
    Economy Research Center, p. 213.
*The amount listed for 1984 was for the first six months ($1 = 800 won).

dependents, but they also support the education of employees themselves. As mentioned earlier in Chapter 7, Hanjin Group has established
an in-house industrial college so that employees with high school diplomas will earn college degrees, and their salary levels and promotional
opportunities will be adjusted according to guidelines for college graduate employees. Employees attend classes after work, and they earn
degrees in just two years.

Samsung Group also has an educational support system consisting of
an in-house college, graduate school, and technical school. Daewoo
Group established a regular technical college, which provides training
not only to their own employees but also to nonemployees. They grant
leaves of absence for their employee-students and scholarship recipients.
Hyundai Group also opened an in-house technical college for their
employees, awarding degrees upon graduation comparable to technical
college degrees. There are also many other corporations who run in-
house educational institutions for their employees.

Organizations also fulfill their social responsibilities by donating
money to various causes. They donate mostly to colleges and universities,
political groups, and social organizations, such as the Boy Scouts. The
donations of Daewoo Group, for example, are shown in Table 12.2. The
amount of donations reached $17,763,108 at the exchange rate of $1 to
800 won in the first six months of 1984, including $812,500 for the Ilhae
Foundation of the then president, Chun Doo Hwan.

According to a survey of 635 corporations by the Korean Efficiency
Association (A Survey 1992), a total of 879.6 billion won ($1.173 billion
at the exchange rate of $1 to 750 won) was spent in 1991 for the employee
benefits by these corporations and represents an increase of 30.7 percent
from the previous year. Since Rho Tae Woo became president of South
Korea, employees have enjoyed relative freedom in organizing labor
unions and expressing their viewpoints towards management. Employers

Table 12.2
Donations of Daewoo Group (In Thousand Won)

	1980	1981	1982	1983	1984
Research funds	1,800	48,000	36,000	44,839	100,000
Scholarships	38,828	396,648	615,991	84,391	6,352
Donations to schools	1,346,245	1,410,658	1,511,578	2,466,774	1,217,399
Employees' children	N.A.	N.A.	52,041	78,359	50,664
Donations to social groups	111,901	768,252	567,246	210,329	693,867
Community development	21,650	663,895	1,090,631	1,162,814	306,725
Environmental protection	1,000	4,500	2,480	2,600	11,100,000
Cultural activities	549,390	14,890	5,410	150,000	96,640
Sports	59,500	85,340	34,530	54,210	638,840
Total	2,138,314	3,392,383	3,915,907	4,254,316	14,210,487

Source: Song, I. S. (1984). *Social Services of Corporations* (in Korean). Seoul: The Korean
    Economy Research Center.
Note: The figures listed for 1984 are for the first six months.

have also expanded employee benefits to maintain a satisfactory labor–
management relationship along with the reciprocal principle.

ETHICAL ISSUES

Ethical, social, and economic practices are very serious issues in South
Korea. Extensive unethical behavior in Korea is so serious that a Blue
House (the equivalent of the United States White House in South Korea)
meeting was held in March 1991 (Bae 1991). Government officials reported
many examples of unethical business behaviors and expressed their
concern that these unethical business dealings would result in weaken-
ing competitiveness.

Asian Business of Hong Kong published an article on the corruption
in South Korea according to Lee (1990). The article indicated that cor-

ruption had become an integral part of Korean business, and that it was crucial for international corporations to learn how to deal with this corruption. The article expressed the belief that government officials are the "godfathers" of corruption and advised South Korean businesses to enhance international competitiveness by overcoming this corruption (Lee 1990).

The following is an example of how corruption and bribery work in the construction industry (Chang 1992). In Pusan, Korea, Mr. Lee was going to build a five-story building of 500 pyong (17,850 square feet). He filed an application for a building permit and was rejected by the official on the grounds that the application form was not completed. He applied again, but the official still did not grant a permit. His building designer hinted that he must give 1,000 won per pyong to the official to obtain a building permit. So he gave 500,000 won ($641 at the exchange rate of $1 to 780 won) to the official and obtained the building permit.

Before he could start construction, Mr. Lee had to give 100,000 won ($128) to the fire station officials to obtain a fire protection permit. He then gave money to the city construction officials to report his construction. Next, he gave 100,000 won to the police box in the precinct, and he gave money to the police officer who visited his construction site each month until the construction was completed. When one local government official approached him, he gave him 100,000 won, and an additional 100,000 won each for two inspections. After the construction, he had to give 800,000 won ($1,026) again to the fire station to obtain their final approval and 1,500,000 won ($1,923) to the construction office of the city government to obtain a certificate of completion for his building.

Unethical corruption and bribery are not confined to South Korea. They have been practiced everywhere and at every time. In the Book of Exodus in the Old Testament, we read, "Find some capable, godly, honest men who hate bribes, and appoint them as judges" (18:21). This verse implied that bribery existed even in ancient Israel.

The United States is no exception to this practice of bribery. A local newspaper in South Carolina (State Grand Jury 1992, p. 1) reported, "The state grand jury has leveled bribery charges against three owners of a Seneca-based construction company and has detailed 'alarming' accounts of how the firm rewarded Highway Department employees." In a different article, the newspaper also reported, "The state Highway Department has suffered for years from influence-peddling through cash payments, trips and gifts, even though employees were warned not to accept them, a state grand jury report says. The report was issued after the state grand jury returned indictments against six people charging them with bribery or ethical violations" (Highway Department 1992, p. 1).

The Wall Street Journal (Jacobs 1985, p. 13C) reported, "To countless small businesses, cheating Uncle Sam is as routine as making the payroll and marketing the product." The Wall Street Journal (Allen 1988, p. 19R) also reported, "Prof. William Baxter of the Stanford Law School notes that for such owners, delayed building permits or failed sanitation inspections can be 'life-threatening events' that make them cave in to bribe demands."

Japan also has problems with ethical issues. According to Newsweek (Powell and Takayama 1992), Noboru Takeshida, the former prime minister, admitted that he had received $1.2 million from a Tokyo company. He was disgraced by the so-called Recruit scandal and was also obliged to testify on the Sagawa Kyubin Affair, a political scandal. Shin Kanemaru, titular chairman of Takeshida's faction, admitted accepting $4 million from Hiroyasu Watanabe, president of Tokyo Kyubin Co., a large parcel delivery firm with reputed ties to Japan's mob.

Korean society under the teachings of Confucianism strongly emphasizes moral and ethical behavior. The Koreans are taught by their parents to practice the right way, with virtuous and moral behavior (tao te). There are many Koreans who strictly abide by moral and ethical standards, so it is very unfortunate to see corruption, bribery, and unethical behaviors in the Korean management system.

There is, however, a nuance of culture between the United States and South Korea. When we were invited as guest speakers for professional meetings and college classes in South Korea, we were presented with a white envelope containing a certain amount of cash or a check as an honorarium or expression of appreciation, and "a token of gratitude" was written on the envelope. However, when we invite guest speakers to our classes here in the United States, no cash, check, or honorarium is presented to them as a token of appreciation. In most cases, the guest speakers do not expect any monetary rewards for their contribution, yet they connect their current presentation to their professional development for future salary increase and promotion. In other words, they receive nothing today, but expect to receive extrinsic rewards tomorrow. The Koreans behave differently. They receive their rewards today, and do not link the activity to the future. A Korean professor, for example, receives money, but does not connect the activity to professional development on his or her resume. Korean-American professors in the United States act like a hybrid of these two different cultures by accepting an honorarium for lecturing in South Korea, while viewing the lecture as a professional activity for a promotion and salary increase at their American institutions.

Of course, we are well aware that there are frequent cases of honorariums paid to guest speakers inside and outside classroom lectures in the United States. Some invited speakers even demand $25,000 for each talk. However, there are also many cases where guest speakers do not expect anything for their talks. In South Korea, this is not the case: Guest speakers always receive an anticipated honorarium.

Giving a tip is not commonly practiced in South Korea. No service providers, such as taxi drivers and waitresses, expect tips from their customers for their services. However, tipping is a common practice in the United States as a token of appreciation for services rendered. Assume that some Korean visitors to the United States ignored this cherished American custom. Were they engaged in unethical behavior? The answer is "yes" according to the American standard, but it has nothing to do with ethical issues to Koreans. Koreans, however, are advised to comply with the American custom, and they usually tip for services provided when traveling in the United States.

Should Americans on tour or living in South Korea comply with the Korean tradition of not giving tips for services rendered, or should they practice the American custom of giving tips in South Korea? Should Americans, who pride themselves as civilized people by giving tips, show contempt for Koreans as uncivilized people? Ethical issues, in principle, are universally applicable ones; however, there seem to be some subtle areas where ethical issues are more culture-bound.

The Korean practice of giving a white envelope with money in it is not correctly understood in the Western world. In most cases, it is a token of appreciation, congratulation, or sympathy, rather than bribery since the Koreans prefer cash to gifts. Traditionally, they congratulate the family members, relatives, friends, and job-related members at a wedding ceremony by giving cash in a white envelope. This tradition equally applies to a house of mourning. Koreans visit the house of the deceased and express their condolence to the family members of the deceased by giving a white envelope with money in it.

A few years ago, I (the female author of this book) sent a check of $100 to an American lady simply because she helped me to adjust to the United States during my first few years in this country. I have never forgotten the help I received from her. Later she told me that she was so upset about the money she received that she almost decided to return it. In many situations, receiving cash is not a culturally accustomed behavior in America. Yet my intention was honest, and I sent the check as a token of true appreciation.

We are sometimes puzzled by one particular practice of Americans (at least in this region of the deep South). When an American sends a gift to either a high school or a college graduate, usually it is a check for $10 or more in an envelope. Among the immediate family members in South Korea, senior members of the family (uncles and aunts) usually give cash (not even in a white envelope) to their juniors (young nephews and nieces) as a token of their love. The Koreans are, therefore, accustomed to a cash gift in the form of a white envelope with money in it, and at least this practice is not a quid pro quo as it seems in America.

This traditional practice of the Koreans, however, can be easily extended to bribery. Sometimes it is hard to distinguish whether the money presented is for appreciation or for bribery, since the money may serve both purposes. Some Koreans hand out cash or white envelopes with money inside to most government (federal, state, or local) officials for permits, licenses, and other businesses. The Korean management system as a part of the Korean society is not immune to this vicious practice. Sometimes entrepreneurs and managers are helpless. They must donate huge sums of money as a political contribution merely for their very survival. When a company obtains a loan from a bank, the company is obliged to give back a certain amount of money to the loan officials as a form of commission.

In the Korean management system, the ethical issue is very serious in that unethical business practices eventually weaken the competitiveness of enterprises. However, unethical business practices will prevail for several reasons.

The Lifestyle of Koreans

As was discussed previously, the cash gift has become an integral part of the Korean social behavior. When Koreans appreciate something, they give cash as in the case of guest speakers in classrooms. When Koreans celebrate, they give cash as in the case of a wedding, although other gifts besides cash are given occasionally. When a Korean consoles another Korean for a loss of kin, he or she again gives cash. Therefore, when Koreans give cash to government officials for some favors, they do not engage in extensive moral self-struggle simply because giving cash is a familiar pattern of life.

Government-Business Relations

As long as the government has a strong impact on and interferes with both business and nonbusiness, none of them can avoid political contribution, an essential to their very survival. This statement is more valid for business enterprises than for nonbusiness organizations because they are money makers. Refusing to donate to government leaders and ruling politicians is simply a suicidal action. Political donations are ethical and legal up to a point, and become unethical only if excessive contributions are involved, even though it is usually a give and take situation. In most cases, businesses donate huge sums of money as part of their business strategy for survival and growth. To stay alive, a businessman is forced to be unethical.

Government Laws and Regulations

There are many laws and regulations that require licenses, permits, and inspections, and one can meet many legal requirements through normal (ethical) practices. However, when this process is delayed by government officials for uncertain reasons, it may be a signal to applicants that someone is demanding additional money beyond the set legal fees, and are forced to give additional money to the officials. This is clearly an unethical act of bribery both for the officials and the applicant.

Competition

Competition often drives both business and nonbusiness people to unethical behavior. In a capitalist society, survival of the fittest reigns supreme. A business person has to beat his or her competitors, and means may seem to justify ends in this case. Honesty in business dealings may not be assured, consumers may be deceived or cheated, investors may be swindled, or business traders may be deprived of sales by devious competitors (Wilcox 1966). Unethical behavior may simply be an integral part of capitalism. As a result, unethical behavior of Koreans in their capitalist society is not a unique phenomenon. Perhaps a businessman has to be unethical to be competitive in a capitalist society.

Nonguilt Culture

According to Fr. Karl Huber (Spring 1992), one European cultural heritage is the absolute transcendence of God. This implies that Westerners (Europeans and Americans) strive to behave according to the intention of God. A strong ethical society has developed in the Western world whereby if someone fails to meet the demands of God, he or she feels guilty for a sin against Him. In this society, there is a clear-cut line between ethical and unethical behavior.

Traditionally, Koreans have never developed a guilt or sin culture because there is no concept of the absolute transcendence of God. As long as someone honors laws and cultural norms, he or she is a good citizen and does not need to struggle with guilt or sin beyond human conscience. In fact, although the Koreans are taught to conduct a virtuous life, there is no clear distinction in Korean society between unethical and ethical behavior, as in the Western society. Rather, there is a gray and overlapping area of ethical and unethical behavior in Korean society, at least from the perspective of Western society.

Japan's situation is similar to South Korea's. Sterngold (1992) reported that Japanese politicians received cash, but they denied it as a bribe. Therefore, it seems that the Japanese also maintain a gray area of ethical behavior, as do the Koreans.

The Linking-Pin

As was discussed in Chapter 6, the Koreans behave through FAR (family, alumni, and regionalism) for their career success in the Korean management system, and through this network of connections, they help one another. This system often works constructively, but it can also work destructively.

It is not an easy process to obtain government licenses and permits for a business or to pass various inspections, so in many cases, the applicant uses the connections of FAR to achieve these goals. The applicant usually can locate one member of FAR who is close to those government officials who have the authority to grant licenses or permits. This member then acts like a linking-pin between the applicant and the government official(s). Instead of handing a white envelope with money inside directly to the government official, the applicant delivers the money to the linking-pin who, in turn, gives the money to the government official. In many cases, the linking-pin person becomes an intermediary, purely for friendship or special relation gratis, between government officials and the applicants. It is apparently an unethical behavior. However, by using the linking-pin, the Koreans are able to justify their behavior because they did not participate directly in unethical behavior.

Poorly Defined Life Pattern

Americans strive hard to honor civil rights by changing many expressions like "chairman" to "chairperson." Likewise, instead of using the term "he," Americans use "he or she" as a personal pronoun. In English, there is a clear distinction of gender. In Korea, however, there are no terms meaning "chairman" and "chairlady." There is only one expression of "chairperson," the term "person" signifying both "male" and "female." No pronouns expressing "he" or "she" exist in the Korean vocabulary.

There is a clear distinction in every aspect of life in the United States because Americans demand it. Unethical behavior is clearly distinguished from ethical behavior, and there is no overlap between them. In South Korea, the world is not so clearly defined as it is to Americans. Koreans definitely distinguish unethical behavior from ethical behavior. Through their unclarified living pattern, however, a neutralizing force between these two conflicting phenomena intervenes in their lives. This neutralizing force somewhat allows unethical behavior, the linking-pin case discussed above being a typical example.

In conclusion, both business and non-business organizations in the Korean management system have awesome social responsibilities to perform, and entrepreneurs, managers, and leaders of these organizations understand it perfectly. In business, business managers fulfill their social responsibilities by aiming at producing profit because the

Korean economy needs fast economic growth. However, the direction of business's social responsibility has shifted somewhat since the Rho Tae Woo government took office. Business managers have concentrated on improving the well-being of their employees as a historic trend along with other social responsibility. The Korean managers are under heavy pressure to balance two seemingly conflicting objectives: producing profit and fulfilling social responsibility.

In the Korean management system, the unethical behavior of managers and leaders is a serious problem. Although they may insist that ethical issues should not be measured by the Western standards alone, they justify their behavior from an ethical point of view. We agree that there exists some gray areas in ethical issues in the Korean management system because of their unique cultural heritage. Still, we strongly believe that the Koreans have a responsibility to clarify and redefine these gray areas to the rest of the global community in order to enhance their competitiveness.

REFERENCES

A Survey of Employee Benefits. The Korean Efficiency Association, 1992.

Allen, M. Small-business Jungle. *The Wall Street Journal* (June 10, 1988).

Bae, I. J. Wrong-doings in Business Will Result in Weakness in Competitiveness. *The Dong-A Daily News* (March 30, 1991).

Chang, I. C. Without Money Envelope, No Building Construction. *The Dong-A Daily News* (February 18, 1992).

Davis, K., and Blomstrom, R. L. *Business, Society, and Environment.* 4th ed., chap. 3. New York: McGraw-Hill, 1980.

Freedman, M. *Capitalism and Freedom.* Chicago: University of Chicago, 1962.

Highway Department Suffering from Influence-Peddling: Report. *The Index-Journal* (November 19, 1992).

Huber, K. Fr. Economic Growth and the Common Good in Christian Social Doctrine. *Ethics & International Affairs* (Spring, 1992).

Jacobs, S. L. Hide and Sneak. *The Wall Street Journal* (May 20, 1985).

Kim, C. H. The Repressive Impact of Unemployment. *The Hankuk Daily News* (November 13, 1992).

Kim, S. U. Female Government Officials and Higher Positions. *The Dong-A Daily News* (April 4, 1991).

Lee, Y. K. You Must Learn about Corruption to Engage in Business in South Korea. *The Dong-A Daily News* (March 8, 1990).

Paying Fines is Cheaper Than Environment Cleaning Costs. *The Dong-A Daily News* (December 12, 1992).

Powell, B., and Takayama, H. A Kingmaker on the Line. *Newsweek* (November 30, 1992).

State Grand Jury Indicts Thrifts. *The Index-Journal* (November 19, 1992).

Sterngold, J. Japanese Say They Got Cash but It Wasn't a "Bribe." *The New York Times* (February 26, 1992).

Wilcox, C. *Public Policies Toward Business.* Homewood, Ill.: Richard D. Irwin, Inc., 1966.

Epilogue

Two important events occurred in December 1992 in South Korea: the presidential election on December 18 and the college entrance examination on December 22. These events will once again explain the features of the Korean culture and their impact on the Korean management system.

When we were writing this epilogue, Kim Young Sam, the presidential candidate from the ruling government party, was elected president of South Korea with 41.4 percent of the general votes. Kim Dae Jung, an arch-rival of Kim Young Sam, finished second with 33.3 percent, and Chung Ju Yung, an ex-*chaebol* tycoon of Hyundai Group, finished third with 16.1 percent (Result 1992). Kim Young Sam promoted change with stability, a very conservative approach. Kim Dae Jung, on the other hand, emphasized growth with reformation aiming at an equitable society, a relatively radical approach in South Korea. Chung Ju Yung insisted that only someone who was successful in business could be an effective president and promised to dissolve all chaebol group organizations. To these three candidates, the economic issue was one of the major issues for their presidential campaign.

This presidential election was a critical one for chaebol and other major corporations because the three main presidential contenders disclosed different economic policies, which would have a significant impact on their business operations. The election was critical for the Korean management system because the system could be redefined, reformed, reorganized, or remain the same depending on which presidential candidate would be elected.

In the South Korean management system, government and business developed a unique quid pro quo (see Chapter 3). As a result, most chaebol corporations focused their attention on gathering reliable information on the outcome of the presidential election. Some major chaebol groups devised three different scenarios for the three presidential candidates, one for each candidate relating the major economic policy to his business strategies.

The election of Kim Young Sam as the next president has significant implications for South Korean management. His major economic policy proposal promotes change with stability, which means maintaining a status quo without significant changes. In other words, this election demonstrated a Korean conservative trend. They rejected the rather radical policy of Kim Dae Jung as well as the control of the chaebol boss of Chung Ju Yung over government, business, and politics.

The election also brought a significant change to the norms of the Koreans, which may have a significant impact on the Korean management system. The Koreans traditionally consider a politician as traitor when he or she changes to the ruling party from the opposition party. Kim Young Sam did exactly that as part of his grand strategy for the 1992 presidential election. Historically, he would have been condemned as a traitor by the Koreans who abide by principles. Instead, he was elected president of South Korea, signifying that the Koreans are gradually accepting the importance of compromise.

Another implication of the election is related to religion. As was mentioned in Chapter 1, Kim Young Sam is a Presbyterian elder, a devout Christian. The Koreans elected him president, even though the majority of Koreans belong to Oriental religions, such as Buddhism, Confucianism, and Shamanism. After he was elected president, Kim officially announced that he would help promote Buddhism for a balanced growth of religions (Kim Emphasizes Cooperation 1992). This election reaffirms a cherished tradition of the Korean culture—peaceful coexistence of various religions—although some radically ultrafundamental Christians are threatening to disturb other religions. There need not be any specific civil rights regulations for various religious believers in the Korean management system, because each religion is accepted and treated fairly.

Although Kim Young Sam was elected president, there were indications that it is imperative to redefine the relationship between the government and chaebol groups (see Chapter 6). It surfaced when Chung Ju Yung, a former chaebol tycoon of Hyundai, challenged vigorously the ruling party and Kim Young Sam, their presidential candidate. Both candidates engaged in a dog fight during the campaign because the encroachment of Chung was sure to give an unearned advantage to Kim Dae Jung, an arch-rival of Kim Young Sam. In various ways, the South Korean government suppressed Hyundai Group of Chung Ju Yung. Some of the Hyundai executives were arrested for possible violations of the election law; the Internal Revenue Service engaged Hyundai in a tax audit; and the giant Hyundai Group experienced hardship in raising needed capital. In addition to the pressure from the government, the operation of Hyundai

Group was paralyzed because employees engaged either directly or indirectly in the campaign for Chung Ju Yung by ignoring their daily business tasks. Some of the presidents of Hyundai Group even proposed to close some of their group corporations, but finally decided to keep them open.

If he were elected president of South Korea, Chung Ju Yung promised to dissolve chaebol groups, directly reflecting the sentiment of the Koreans toward them. They are keenly aware that these chaebol groups have been the driving force for an impressive economic growth of South Korea and that they owe chaebol groups for their jobs and a significant increase in the standard of living. However, they are becoming uneasy about their power and dominance in every aspect of South Korea, not only in business and economy.

The destiny of chaebol groups will be decided by the redefinition of government-chaebol group relations. A course of action may be that chaebol groups will consolidate their formidable power to influence politics to enable them to grasp both political and economic power in South Korea. It is ironic that the emergence of Chung Ju Yung as a powerful political figure acknowledges the aggressive approach of chaebol groups, even though he promised their dissolution. The chaebol groups, however, have to reassess this approach because the Korean people rejected both Chung himself and an attempt by chaebol groups to dominate economy and politics.

The second course of action may be that the government will put more pressure on chaebol groups to weaken their power. Unless this movement brings an adverse impact on economic growth, it will be a more desirable policy than others because it will contribute to achieving an equitable society in South Korea. Small businesses, for example, who have been at the mercy of chaebol corporations, will have a stronger voice for their interests.

There will be no drastic change in the relationship between the government and chaebol groups under the Kim Young Sam government, because he promised to maintain traditional ways of doing business. However, there will be some small but significant change because the chaebol groups strongly oppose the hush-money political contribution to the government and ruling political leaders. At the same time, the Korean people demand the restraint of the formidable power of the chaebol groups. In the next five years when Kim Young Sam is president of South Korea, the relationship between the government and chaebol groups will be redefined one way or another.

December 22, 1992 was also a crucial day for the Korean society and the Korean management system—the day of the college entrance examination. We have explained throughout this book the importance of education to Koreans. They firmly believe that their career success depends upon their level of education. Most parents are almost desperate to send their children through a four-year college. According to a survey of the Education Policy Advisory Council to the president (A Consciousness Survey 1992), 96.5 percent of parents want to send their sons to college, and 93.7 percent of them want to send their daughters to college. In one sense, South Korea is a country of education zealots, since whether or not a high school graduate is admitted to a (prestigious) college is a matter of life or death. School children prepare for this examination as early as possible with the total support of their parents, mostly their mothers.

December 22, 1992 was really a D-day for the Koreans. The government ordered all organizations (private and public) and various schools with more than 50 employees in the 15 major metropolitan areas to open their offices after 10 a.m. to facilitate the traffic of applicants for the college examination, and bus companies were ordered to reschedule their buses to run exclusively between 6:00 a.m. and 8:00 a.m. Subways were rescheduled to run more frequently between 6:00 a.m. and 10:00 a.m., and a special train of 18 cars ran for the college applicants from remote areas (Delays 1992). Police patrol cars were encouraged to pick up college applicants and deliver them to examination sites, (see the Introduction for the related story), and police stations offered lodging for those who could not find hotels. It was a day of national mobilization since education is a deadly serious issue in South Korea.

When I visited Seoul, South Korea, a few years ago, I stayed two weeks at my sister-in-law's house. The family had two sons: One was a high school junior, and the other was a ninth-grade student. They continually studied for the college entrance examination, which would take place in a few years. I was given a door key to avoid disturbing their studies by ringing the door bell and was advised not to have outsiders call when the boys were studying because the telephone ring and subsequent talk would interfere with their studies. I was also asked to talk in hushed tones at home in order not to disturb their studies. Likewise, the parents of the students kept their television set in their bedroom and kept the tone very low so that it would not disturb their sons. Except for sleeping hours, they allocated all day for their studies at school, at home, and sometimes at tutoring institutions. My sister-in-law has attended the prayer meeting at 4:00 a.m. everyday in her church to pray for her eldest son's college admission on December 22, 1992. I sensed that the whole universe revolved around the studies of the two sons in that family.

This phenomenon is not confined to this family alone. All Korean families share a similar experience. As was mentioned in Chapter 1, it is a very touching scene when mothers in their forties and fifties prayed devoutly, hour after hour despite the cold winter weather, in the outside yard of Buddhist temples for their children's college admission. This is another reason why the examination day is a big social event in South Korea. Each year, this phenomenon repeats itself.

It was, therefore, not an accident when the Korean students scored highest in math and science among the participating countries for the International Assessment of Education Progress (IAEP) tests administered by the Educational Testing Service, which also runs the Scholastic Aptitude Tests (SATs) (Roser 1992; Kantrowitz and Wingert 1992).

This Korean zeal for education has significant implications to the Korean management system. It also explains the phenomenal economic growth since the 1960s in South Korea. One of the most important implications is that the Korean management system has been blessed with a continuous supply of dedicated and highly educated personnel. These educated Koreans have become either innovative entrepreneurs or effective and productive managers and employees in the Korean management system. The education and management system combination is one of the most important contributors to the stunning achievements of the Korean economy.

This trend will continue in the foreseeable future unless some extremely unexpected events occur. Since the mid-1980s, graduates of technical high schools have achieved 100 percent employment, and more than 80 percent of technical college graduates have succeeded in finding jobs. At the same time, four-year college or university graduates have experienced difficulty in locating jobs, and just 50 percent of them succeeded in locating jobs in 1992. This trend induced the government to change its education policy. The government planned to change the ratio between technical high schools and general high schools from 32:68, respectively, to 50:50 through a five-year plan that was started in 1990 (Sons with 96.5% 1992). This trend may alleviate the experience of the so-called "examination hell" high school graduates bear during the four-year college admission process. Yet Koreans will try to advance to four-year (prestigious) universities not only for their future career success, but also to enhance their family prestige and pride (see Chapter 6).

Some scholars strongly criticize the existing education system in South Korea, which focuses exclusively on the college entrance examination. Their rationale is that by focusing on the college entrance examination, the Korean education system forgoes a well-rounded education, and it ignores the development of students' creativity. Having experienced both the education systems of South Korea and the United States, we would like to emphasize that both systems will benefit significantly by learning a lesson from each other. However, it is clear that Korean parents will never abandon their emphasis on the education of their children.

No management system remains static. Since we are living in a world of constant change, management systems must adapt to these changes for survival and prosperity. The American management system, for example, has been changed into a more team-oriented management system by using employee empowerment. American business organizations have become more lean and mean by restructuring and laying off employees. This process of adjustment is necessary so that a management system can maintain its competitive edge in the global economy. Yet the American management system maintains its mainframe structure, which distinguishes itself from other management systems.

Likewise, the Korean management system will undergo constant change to adapt to the ever-changing environment. However, the mainframe structure of the Korean management system will remain the same to distinguish itself from other management systems, some of which we have tried to identify throughout this book. However, some changes are inevitable.

Changes of Some Cultural Elements

As the standard of living improves and interaction with other countries increases, some cultural elements will change. Trends toward the nuclear family will be intensified, and traditional multigeneration family systems will yield to these trends. There will also be changes in behavioral patterns, based on Korean culture. As was discussed in Chapter 5, relationships with high school classmates are critically important to the behavior of the Koreans and the implication to the Korean management system. Recently, however, the importance of college classmates has increased in both business and nonbusiness organizations (College Classmates 1992). College classmates are becoming more important because they are able to maintain job-related relationships, while high school classmates are maintaining pure friendships without job-related connotations. In the industrialized society of South Korea, the job-oriented relationship is gaining more importance than the mere friendship-oriented relationship.

Improvement of Women's Rights in the Korean Management System

The Korean society has been a male-dominated society. However, this trend will change drastically in the future because the society has been forced by law to change this practice. According to the Equal Employment Act, effective in October 1992, any discrimination toward women will be prosecuted, and two-year prison sentences and fines will be forced upon the convicted (Discrimination Against Women 1992).

Samsung Group, one of the largest chaebol, already complied with this law by adopting a policy not to discriminate against women in recruiting, department assignments, and promotions. Only 4 percent of the recruits at Samsung Group were women in the past, but this figure will increase to 20 percent in the near future (Equal Opportunity 1992). Traditionally, chaebol groups recruited women only for specified fields. It remains to be seen whether the Korean management system will really provide equal employment by gender. Even in the United States, there still exists a glass ceiling for women and other minority groups.

Change of Working Habits

As was discussed in Chapter 7, the Koreans work long hours by world standards. However, the attitudes of the Korean employees are somewhat in a transformation process from work ethics to leisure ethics. Young workers these days decline to work overtime; instead, they favor spending more time with their family and friends. Some workers even seek employment based on their not having to work overtime and at night. The Korean management system will begin to comply with the needs and demands of employees. Korean entrepreneurs and top executives are keenly aware that the autocratic, dictatorial days are gone forever from the Korean management system, yet some of the executives have lamented that the Korean society has become a leisure ethic society too soon, and that South Korea needs more hard work and longer working hours.

Introduction of a Merit System to the Korean Management System

As we also discussed in Chapter 7, the Korean management system depends heavily on the seniority system for human resources management. This system has the definite advantage of maintaining stability in organizations. However, among its clear disadvantages are a lack of motivation and a sense of achievement.

To overcome this problem, some chaebol groups have applied the merit bonus system to attract employees' innovative contributions. Samsung and Hyundai are two examples. Samsung Group provides 300,000 to 400,000 won ($375 to $500 at the exchange rate of $1 to 800 won) as a merit bonus for employees whose performances were outstanding, in addition to the end-of-year bonus of 270 percent of the regular monthly salary, as mentioned in Chapter 7. Hyundai Group pays up to 140 percent as a merit bonus to some manufacturing employees, in addition to the regular end of the year bonus of 100 to 300 percent. The merit bonus system enhances productivity and motivation, but nevertheless, some problems are inherent in this system as evidenced by its application in the United States (see Chapter 7).

The Encounter of the Korean Management System with Dreadful Challenges Inside and Outside

The South Korean economy seems to be at the crossroads, and its future direction is uncertain. One possibility is that the economy will grow more, and that South Korea will become a fully industrialized country around the turn of the 21st century. The other possibility—albeit gloomy—is that the South Korean economy will become stagnant by losing its competitive edge. Already there are some signs of a growth slowdown. According to the Bank of Korea (Third-Quarter Trend 1992), the third-quarter economic growth in 1992 was a mere 3.1 percent, the lowest in 11 years. Of course, this low percentage of economic growth is a result of the stability policy of the government.

The South Korean economy will be an economy sandwiched among the advanced countries of Japan, the United States, and some European countries, as well as among the late-starting developing countries, and it will be an uphill task to catch up to the advanced countries. Although the gap is narrowing, the process is very slow. The late-starting countries, such as Malaysia, Thailand, Indonesia, and China, are catching up with such alarming speed that the South Korean economy has become restless.

In order to overcome these threatening problems, the South Korean management system must develop some drastic strategies for maintaining its competitive edge. One strategy is to increase the productivity, quality, and development of new products and services. Again, there is a dangerous red light here. According to the survey of the Korean Trade Public Corporation (A Survey 1992), more than one-half of the Japanese buyers who stopped importing from South Korea explained their actions on the grounds of the poor quality of goods. The Japanese buyers also complained that Korean goods were more expensive than goods from Hong Kong and Taiwan. Unless the Korean corporations improve their quality, upgrade their productivity, and develop new products, it will be difficult for them to free themselves from a sandwiched economy.

As a way of attacking these pending problems, many Korean enterprises have joined with developing countries for direct investments and joint ventures in Thailand, Malaysia, Indonesia, and extensively in China. At the same time, some Korean corporations have established joint ventures with American companies. Hyundai Group, for example, has a computer plant in the United States for access to the most recent technology and information (see Chapter 6). Japan is very reluctant to offer technology to South Korea, and some Korean businessmen lament that many Korean factories merely assemble the parts imported from Japan and make them into finished products. This is one of the basic reasons for the widening gap in the trade imbalance between Japan and South Korea.

Another method is to develop a grand Northern policy. This economic policy includes those countries located to the north of South Korea: North Korea, China, Mongolia and Central Asian Republics, and Russia (Nakarmi, Brady, and Curry 1992). Daewoo Group has plans to invest $90 million in the area, excluding China and North Korea and also has an ambitious plan to invest in North Korea, once the investment environment is favorable. Other major chaebol corporations are now actively seeking the possibility of investment in this Northern region. Their investments, of course, depend on the political climate of this very unstable area.

It remains to be seen whether the South Korean management will successfully challenge the unpredictable future as it did in the past. It also remains to be seen whether South Korea will contribute to upgrading the Korean economy and the standard of living of the Korean people. The Koreans collectively have a strong aspiration to become a member of developed countries such as the Group of Seven (G7) who are Canada, France, Germany, Italy, Japan, the United Kingdom, and the United States. Korean businessmen overcame many crises, such as the oil crisis of the 1970s (see Chapter 4) and turned them around to their advantage. If the past is any guide, despite uncertain domestic and global environments, there are reasons for cautious optimism about the future of the Korean management system.

At the time of the printing of this book, Kim Young Sam has been president of South Korea for six months. During this time, he has taken drastic and courageous measures in fighting the corruption that plagued the Korean society by declaring the Anti-Corruption Proclamation. Corrupt politicians, government officials, generals, admirals, high-ranking military officers, and some businessmen have been purged ruthlessly. Many of them were arrested for their corruption and put into jail.

President Kim proclaimed that he would not accept any political contributions from anyone—including chaebol groups—and warned politicians and government officials not to take contributions and bribes. The Korean people have enthusiastically supported the cleaning effort of the president by showing 70 to 80 percent support. Koreans call this phenomenon a "Reformation Mania."

In Chapter 12 we discussed the ethical issues of the Korean management system and reviewed the grave problem of unethical practices in the system. We also emphasized that these unethical practices must be eliminated to maintain a competitive edge in the global competition. It is yet to be seen whether the Korean society and the Korean management system will be relatively corruption-free, even though we have some reservations about it since the culture and behavioral patterns of the Koreans may interfere somewhat with such cleansing efforts.

Chaebol groups have been very uneasy with the new government mainly because they were not exactly certain of the government policy of President Kim Young Sam toward chaebol groups. The new government has often sent somewhat conflicting signals toward chaebol. Sometimes the president emphasizes self-regulation of chaebol groups by removing and reforming many of the restrictive government measures. At other times, the government interferes with chaebol groups by urging them to invest more now. Again, it remains to be seen how the mighty chaebol groups will be redefined under the Kim government. It is a very delicate issue to balance economic growth and equitable income distribution. Chaebol groups have to be mobilized aggressively to achieve a high economic growth which may result in economic concentration in a few mighty chaebol groups. At the same time, the power of chaebol groups must be weakened to implement equitable income distribution. The Rho Tae Woo government tried and ended with an unsatisfactory result to everyone.

Chung Ju Yung, the founder of Hyundai Group and a presidential candidate, lost his bid. He resigned from his political party which he founded, and cleared himself from politics by resigning from Congress. He apologized to both Kim Young Sam and Kim Dae Jung for accusing them and even advised his followers to resign from his political party, urging them to cooperate with the Kim government. He also promised to concentrate his effort on business, and people speculated that his movement was aimed at minimizing the retaliation from the Kim government. We remind readers about the relationship of government and business in South Korea that was discussed in this book.

Yang Jung Mo, the founder of the dismantled Kukje Group, recently won the court battle to repossess his group. The Constitution Court decided that it was against the Constitution to dissolve any chaebol group by political powers. We discussed that the government can create a chaebol or destroy it overnight with or without reasons because of the precedent set in the case of Kukje Group. It remains to be seen whether the government's power will weaken in manipulating chaebol groups in the future.

REFERENCES

College Classmates Are Becoming Important. *The Hankuk Weekly* (December 7, 1992).

A Consciousness Survey on Education. The Education Policy Advisory Council to the President, 1992.

Delays of Opening Hours for College Examinations. *The Hankuk Daily News* (December 21, 1992).

Discrimination Against Women Bankers will be Prosecuted. *The Dong-A Daily News* (July 15, 1992).

Equal Opportunity for Women at Samsung. *The Dong-A Daily News* (October 28, 1992).

Kantrowitz, B., and Wingert, P. An "F" in World Competition: A Major Test Shows U.S. Students Don't Measure Up. *Newsweek* (February 17, 1992).

Kim Emphasizes Cooperation among Various Religions. *The Dong-A Daily News* (December 29, 1992).

Nakarmi, B., Bradley, R., and Curry, L. Can Korea Unite and Conquer? *Business Week* (November 16, 1992).

Roser, M. A. Smartest U.S. Kids Great at Math, but the Other 90% Are "Rotten." *The State* (February 6, 1992).

Result of Presidential Election. *The Dong-A Daily News* (December 22, 1992).

Sons with 96.5%, Daughters with 93.7%. *The Hankuk Daily News* (December 16, 1992).

A Survey on the Japanese Buyers for Korean Goods. The Korean Trade Public Corporation, 1992.

Third-quarter Trend of GNP Growth. *The Bank of Korea,* 1992.

Index

ABOUT THE AUTHORS

CHAN SUP CHANG is a Professor at Lander University, Greenwood, South Carolina. He is the author of *Japanese Auto Industry and the U.S. Market* (Praeger, 1981) and a contributing author in four books. He has written several articles on Korean conglomerates and entrepreneurs of China, Japan, and Korea.

NAHN JOO CHANG is an Assistant Professor at Lander University, Greenwood, South Carolina. She has presented several papers on the Korean management system.